Ancient Peoples and Places

THE BULGARIANS

General Editor

PROFESSOR GLYN DANIEL

For David, Andrew, Caroline and Elizabeth

ABOUT THE AUTHOR

David Lang read Russian, French and German at St John's College, Cambridge, where he was a Scholar and later, Research Fellow. During World War II he went to Persia and became Acting Vice-Consul at Tabriz. Since 1946 he has led an active and varied academic life: he has held a Rotary International Foundation Fellowship (1948–49), a Senior Fellowship at the Russian Institute of Columbia University, New York (1952–53), and a Visiting Professorship at the University of California, Los Angeles (1964–65). He is currently Professor of Caucasian Studies at the School of Oriental and African Studies, University of London, having joined the staff in 1949, and Warden of Connaught Hall.

Professor Lang is author of The Georgians *(Vol. 51 in the Ancient Peoples and Places series) and of* Armenia: Cradle of Civilization *(1971), among many other publications.*

THE
BULGARIANS

FROM PAGAN TIMES
TO THE
OTTOMAN CONQUEST

David Marshall Lang

62 PHOTOGRAPHS
36 LINE DRAWINGS
 2 TABLES
 5 MAPS

 Westview Press · Boulder, Colorado

THIS IS VOLUME EIGHTY-FOUR IN THE SERIES

Ancient Peoples and Places

GENERAL EDITOR: PROFESSOR GLYN DANIEL

Copyright © 1976 Thames and Hudson Ltd.

First published in 1976 by
Thames and Hudson Ltd., London, England

Published in 1976 in the United States of América by
Westview Press, Inc.
1898 Flatiron Court
Boulder, Colorado 80301
Frederick A. Praeger, Publisher and Editorial Director

Library of Congress Cataloging in Publication Data

Lang, David Marshall.
    The Bulgarians: from pagan times to the Ottoman conquest.
    (Ancient peoples and places)
    Bibliography: p.
    Includes index.
    1. Bulgaria—History—To 1393.   2. Bulgarians.
I. Title.
DR74.L36   1976   949.77'01   76–127
ISBN 0-89158-530-3

Filmset by Keyspools Limited, Golborne, Lancashire, and printed in
Great Britain by Camelot Press Ltd., Southampton.

CONTENTS

List of Illustrations

6

FIGURES

Foreword

This book is very much a labour of love, an attempt to repay the kindness and friendship which my family and I have received from Bulgarians of all walks of life, both in Bulgaria and abroad. My first visit to Bulgaria took place in 1967, when I was primarily concerned, as a specialist in Georgian and Caucasian studies, with studying the medieval Georgian monastery at Bachkovo. I later had the opportunity of visiting several of the Armenian communities in Bulgaria, where representatives of this highly cultured nation have been settled for well over a thousand years.

It soon became clear to me that Bulgaria's medieval art and civilization present a picture of remarkable richness and variety, both in their own right, and as a part of what Professor Obolensky has aptly termed the culture of the Byzantine Commonwealth. It seemed to me that a concise presentation of the main stream of Bulgarian history and cultural life during the First and Second Empires, from about AD 680 to the Turkish conquest of 1393–96, might present considerable interest to the Western reader, especially as Sir Steven Runciman's history of the First Empire has long been out of print.

I am grateful to Professor Glyn Daniel for recommending and to the Publishers for accepting the work for inclusion in their 'Ancient Peoples and Places' series. Dr Vivian Pinto of the School of Slavonic and East European Studies has most unselfishly put me in touch with many of his Bulgarian friends and colleagues, as has Mrs Mercia MacDermott, author of two standard works on Bulgarian history. I owe a particular debt to the Bulgarian Committee for Friendship and Cultural Relations with Foreign Countries, who invited me for two visits to Bulgaria, in 1967 and 1971. Among my hosts in that Committee I single out for special thanks Mrs E. Kamova, and my guide and close friend Mr A. Arsov, with whom I shared many scholarly experiences, and also a few hilarious adventures, after the style of Don Quixote and Sancho Panza. The Committee has kindly sent me many books on Bulgarian history and archaeology, and secured for me permission to reproduce a number of drawings and photographs. The Calouste

Foreword

Gulbenkian Foundation in Lisbon, through the good offices of Mr Robert Gulbenkian, made a generous contribution to my visit to Bulgaria in 1971, which enabled me to visit Armenian churches and other important historical monuments. I am also grateful to Sir William Harpham and the staff of the Great Britain–East Europe Centre for many valuable facilities.

I owe a special debt to Mr Gocho Chakalov of Dragalevtsi and his family for many kindnesses, and also for showing me the antiquities of Sozopol, the ancient Black Sea port. Among many eminent Bulgarian scholars who have encouraged me, I would like to thank especially Academician Vladimir Georgiev; Professor Ivan Duichev; Professor Dimităr Angelov, now Director of the National Archaeological Museum, Sofia; also Professor Veselin Beshevliev, and his talented geographer son, Boyan. Professor N. Todorov, director of the Institute of Balkan Studies, gave me much useful advice, as did his colleague, Madame V. Tăpkova-Zaimova. I am especially grateful to my friends and kind guides in Great Tărnovo, Mr Stefan Tzonev, and his wife Nina. I would like to thank His Excellency the Bulgarian Ambassador in London, Professor Alexander Yankov, and his staff, for their generous help and encouragement.

Miss Nina Clark deserves thanks for typing most of the manuscript, with great care and accuracy.

Having taken up the study of Bulgarian history and civilization rather late, and without the customary apprenticeship, I am conscious that my work cannot be free of errors of fact and interpretation. May I say by way of excuse that my mistakes spring perhaps from an excess of zeal, and a desire to convey to a wider public the special flavour of Bulgarian culture, both ancient and modern!

D.M.L.

9

Chronological Table

Chronological Table

Khan Omurtag founds Preslav	821
Building of Aul of Omurtag	822
Omurtag invades Pannonia	827, 829
Death of Omurtag	831
Accession of Boris-Michael	852
Mission of Cyril and Methodius to Moravia	863
Conversion of Bulgaria to Christianity	864–65
St Cyril dies in Rome	869
Oecumenical Council in Constantinople; Bulgarian Church subordinated to Byzantium	869–70
Life and work of St John of Rila	876–946
Death of Methodius in Moravia; disciples go to Bulgaria	885
Abdication of Knyaz Boris-Michael	889
Accession of Tsar Symeon	893
War with Byzantium	894
Peace treaty signed	897
Golden Age of Old Bulgarian Literature: Preslav school flourishes	c. 900
Renewal of war with Byzantium	912
Death of St Clement of Ohrida	916
Symeon reaches walls of Constantinople	924
Symeon proclaims himself Emperor and Autocrat	925
Independence of Bulgarian Orthodox Church	926
Death of Symeon	927
Magyars invade Bulgaria	934
Tomb of Mostich built, with important Slavonic inscription. Beginnings of Bogomil heresy	950
Diplomatic rupture with Byzantium	965
Russian prince Svyatoslav invades Bulgaria	967
Svyatoslav captures Great Preslav and threatens Constantinople	969
Pechenegs invade Bulgaria	970
Cosmos the Priest denounces the Bogomils	c. 970
Emperor John Tzimiskes defeats Svyatoslav	971
Bulgarian tsar Boris II deposed by Tzimiskes	972
Tsar Samuel assumes Bulgarian imperial title and reigns in Macedonia	993
Samuel seizes northeastern Bulgaria from Byzantines	997
Emperor Basil II recovers Preslav region from Samuel	1001
Bulgarian army annihilated by Basil II: death of Tsar Samuel	1014
Tsar Ivan Vladislav killed at Dyrrachium; end of First Bulgarian Empire	1018

11

Chronological Table

CHAPTER I

The Environment: Land and People

Bulgaria falls, broadly speaking, into four major regions. These are, firstly, the phenomenally fertile northern or Danubian tableland; immediately south of this, the mountain belt of the Balkans or Stara Planina, with its southern extensions and foot-hills, which include the Valley of the Roses; southwards again, the valleys and basins of the Maritsa system, including the great Thracian plain; and lastly, on the southern marchlands, the part of the Rhodope mountain range that lies within Bulgarian territory, including also a northwestern extension converging towards the Balkan chain and taking in the Rila Mountains and Mount Vitosha. There is also a western hill belt adjoining Yugo-slavia, and separated from the Rhodope Mountains proper by the river Struma, which runs southwards to its outlet in Greece, the Gulf of Orfano, in the Aegean.

Though the Danube is traditionally thought of as Bulgaria's northern frontier line, it must be remembered that the medieval Bulgarian Khanate and Empires at the zenith of their power took in substantial areas of Wallachia and Transylvania, and that Khan Krum in the early ninth century maintained a common border with the Holy Roman Empire. At one time, Bulgaria's northwestern frontier was the river Tisza, in present-day Hungary.

THE DANUBE In its lower course, the historic waterway of the Danube flows over Quaternary deposits, covered by river sands and gravels. Its left or northern bank, on the Romanian side, is low, flat and marshy, with numerous small lakes. The right bank, on the Bulgarian side, is crowned by low ridges which make excellent town sites, much utilized by the Romans and Byzantines. Today, the south littoral of the Danube has a number of substantial towns and cities, such as Vidin, the Celtic Dunonia and famous for its Baba Vida castle, also Lom and Svishtov, and further east, Rusé, the Turkish Ruschuk, and Silistra, the Duro-storum of Emperor Trajan. In this region flourish wheat and maize, also sunflowers, sugar-beet, vegetables and fruit.

The Danube delta forms an enormous wilderness of swamps and marshes, extending over about one thousand square miles, and largely covered by tall reeds. Before reclamation work was undertaken in modern times, the silt-laden distributaries of the river would slowly meander through this clogged-up swamp towards the Black Sea. The monotony of this waste land is relieved here and there by isolated elevations covered by oak, beech and willows, many of them marking ancient coast lines.

It was through this lower Danube region that the proto-Bulgar Khan Asparukh and his followers had to pass in the seventh century AD, on their way into the Balkans from the northern Black Sea area. The first proto-Bulgar settlement, indeed, was not far south of the Danube estuary, near the present Nicolițel, in the Romanian Dobrudja. This tract of land, known to the Ancients as Scythia Minor or Scythia Pontica, was once inhabited by Thracians. It is characterized by low mountains, fens and sandy steppes, wind-swept and drought-ridden, but remarkably fertile when irrigated. Here the peasants raise abundant cereal crops, while deposits of copper and coal are found.

Dominating the heart of Bulgaria is the Balkan range or Stara Planina ('Old Mountain'), known to the Ancients as the Haemus. It stretches in a majestic sweep through the middle of the country, from the river Timok in the west to the shore of the Black Sea above Burgas in the east.

THE BALKAN RANGE

The main ridge of the Balkans, jagged and uneven, is fully 600 kilometres long. For altitude, it cannot be compared with the Alps or the Caucasus: the summit of Mount Botev, the highest point, does not rise above 2,376 metres. The crest of the range is rounded and fairly accessible, being covered with meadows. Lush grass in spring and sum-mer affords good pasture for flocks of sheep and herds of cattle, and the more sheltered parts of the range have always been quite densely popu-lated. Below the pasture zone is a forest zone, in which beech predomin-ates, while the foot-hills are excellent for farming. Vast orchards grow on the lower northern slopes of the range, especially in the district of Troyan, famous for its monastery which produces a special kind of plum brandy. Among traditional Balkan trades and professions are those of the wood-cutter, the charcoal burner, the saddler, the smith, and the wood-carver. Other industries carried on from medieval times are the making of woollen goods and embroideries, pottery, cutlery and copper goods.

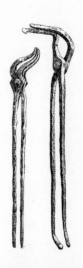

Fig. 1 Pincers and tongs, used by medieval Bulgarian smiths and metalworkers. (After Lishev)

The mountains form an important climatic boundary, warding off masses of cold air pouring down from the north in winter, and causing the Thracian plain to the south to have a much warmer climate than the Danubian plain in the north. A large number of rivers have their source in the Stara Planina, some flowing into the Black Sea, others into the Danube, others again into the Maritsa, which ultimately discharges its waters into the Aegean Sea. As limestone is one of the main rocks of which the Balkan mountains are composed, many caves have formed over the centuries, in some of which there are underground rivers and springs, also stalactites. A picturesque feature to the north of the range is the sinuous valley of the Yantra, which meanders in zigzag fashion through the old capital of Tărnovo, on its way towards the Danube.

The Sredna Gora or 'Anti-Balkan' region comprises a ridge of lower hills running parallel to the main Balkan range, but some miles to the south. Its highest point is the summit of Mount Bogdan (1,604 metres). This Sredna Gora is separated from the Balkans proper by the sub-Balkan depression, a fertile valley area, where lies the town of Kazanluk,

Plates 2, 3   which boasts a painted Thracian tomb. Here are the most extensive rose gardens in the world, which produce attar of roses, one of modern Bulgaria's most valuable products.

THE PLAINS   To the south of the Balkans and Anti-Balkans are two great plains. In western Bulgaria is the wide, flat Sofia plain, overlooked by the massive snow-capped peak of Mount Vitosha. Farther east are the Thracian or Rumelian lowlands, which form a zone of phenomenal fertility stretching between the Anti-Balkans and the Rhodope Mountains, and watered by the river Maritsa and its tributaries. As early as the second millennium BC, this area was extensively settled by the Thracians, who have left large numbers of tumuli dotted all over it. Homer calls Thrace the land of fertility, the mother of fleecy sheep and wonderful horses, which ran in races as swiftly as the wind. Thracian wines were exported to many countries, and the region was the market garden of the Ancient World. Through Thrace runs the river Maritsa, the 'holy Hebros' of Antiquity.

Of exceptional interest is the principal city of the Thracian plain, Plovdiv, known to the Thracians alternatively as Eumolpia or Pulpudeva. It owes its Classical name of Philippopolis to associations with King Philip of Macedon (382–336 BC), who made it one of his frontier posts. The city lies on or between a group of granite crags and hills which rise abruptly out of the flat, fertile plain around. The Romans knew it as Trimontium, after the three principal hills on which the city is built. It is said that 100,000 persons perished when it was captured by the Goths in the third century A D. The Ottoman Turks took Plovdiv in 1364 and, under the name of Filibé, it became the seat of the Beylerbeys of Rumelia.

The Rila Mountains, a northwestern extension of the Rhodope range, are the highest in the entire Balkan peninsula. With its jagged skyline and pointed peaks, the range looks most imposing. The loftiest summit is Mt Moussala (2,925 metres); the name is of Thracian origin, signifying 'the mountain of many streams'. In fact, three of Bulgaria's largest rivers – the Maritsa, the Mesta and the Isker – issue from the upland lakes of the Rila range, an area of high rainfall. These highlands are rich in conifer‚ ous forests, and deer and wild goat are found. The town of Samokov is famous for the craft of wood‚carving, while the Rila monastery, associ‚ ated with St John Rilski, is Bulgaria's leading shrine.

THE SOUTHERN MOUNTAINS

Plates 25–27, 51

Almost as impressive as the Rila Mountains is the Pirin range, immediately to the south, topped by Mt Vihren, or 'peak of wind and storms' (2,915 metres).

Eastwards, in the direction of Turkey, the massif of the Rhodopes is a maze of ridges and valleys. The region's beauty once inspired Ovid, Virgil and Horace, and provided a setting for the myth of Orpheus and Eurydice. Aromatic tobacco grows in the valleys, and the area contains deposits of lead, zinc and other ores. These were being mined by primi‚ tive means already in ancient times. The Rhodope massifs are formed of hard rocks, and their peaks are bare, with old glacial moraines. Quite high up are to be found extensive summer pastures between forests of pine and fir; a little lower down, beech and oak predominate.

Fig. 2

The Rhodope Mountains and the Plovdiv region were the home of the Pomaks or Muslim Bulgarians, who were forcibly converted by the Ottoman Turks, and then became their agents in oppressing the Christians. These Pomaks used to live by wood‚cutting, charcoal‚ burning and other ancient crafts. Also worthy of note is the monastery of Bachkovo in the northern Rhodopes, dating back to the eleventh century, and an active centre of pilgrimage.

Plate 28

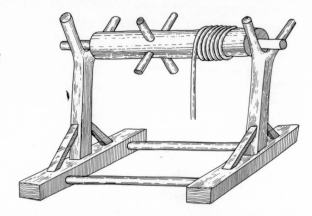

Fig. 2 Medieval Bulgarian mining
winch. (After Lishev)

THE BLACK
SEA COAST
REGION

Especial economic and strategic importance attaches to Bulgaria's 240 miles of Black Sea coast-line. From the seventh century BC Greek colonists from Miletus began settling along this beautiful littoral, to be joined later by others from Chalcedon, Byzantium and Megara. Ports and trading centres grew up at Odessos (Varna), Apollonia (Sozopol), Mesembria (Nessebăr) and Anchialos (Pomorie). These ports were later taken over and extended by the Romans and Byzantines, while Genoese and Venetian merchants favoured them during the Middle Ages. Economic exchanges led in due course to cultural penetration, so that Thrace became a treasure house of Hellenistic and Roman sculpture and art.

Plate 1

TRADE
ROUTES

Bulgaria has always been a focal area for international transport routes. Navigation is possible along the Danube and the Black Sea coast. On land, Bulgaria provides a vital link between the Bosporus and Central Europe, either via Romania, or else by the ancient route through Adrianople (Edirne), Plovdiv, Sofia, Nish and Belgrade. The traveller today follows the same route by car or by Orient Express as the Roman legionary trudged two thousand years ago. Sofia, the ancient Serdica, capital of modern Bulgaria, is situated at the cross-roads of two most important arteries – the east-west route from Istanbul into Serbia and Macedonia, and the north-south route from the Danube towns down to Salonica on the Aegean Sea.

Also worthy of mention is the route from Novae on the Danube which ran in Roman times through Nicopolis ad Istrum (Nikiup) and the Yantra valley via Great Tărnovo, then over the Balkan range by way of the Shipka Pass, across the Valley of the Roses and the Sredna Gora hills. The route passes through the town of Stara Zagora, which was the Thracian Beroe, and the Roman Augusta Traiana, and then south-wards into the Plain of Thrace. In the later Middle Ages, it became the main route linking Tărnovo, the capital, with southern Bulgaria and with Byzantium.

Fig. 16

Rich in fauna and flora, Bulgaria is endowed with a very favourable climate. The average annual temperature is about 12° Centigrade (53° Fahrenheit). In January the average temperature for the whole country is 0° Centigrade (32° Fahrenheit), the northern districts being normally about two degrees colder, the southern lowlands two degrees warmer. Such moderate temperatures suit the growth of autumn-sown crops, also vineyards and orchards. In July, we find an average of 22° Centigrade (72° Fahrenheit). Naturally it is cooler in the high mountains, and hotter on the Thracian plain, or along the Black Sea coast. The average annual rainfall is about 650 litres per square metre; irrigation is widely employed on the plains.

CLIMATE

Among crops which flourish in Bulgaria are tobacco, rice, sesame, aniseed, tomatoes and grapes. Wild flora include many species rare or extinct in other parts of Europe, including unusual types of lavender, pyrethrum and peppermint. The mouths of the Kamchiya, the Ropo-tamo and other rivers flowing into the Black Sea are overgrown with uncommon endemic plant species. Bulgaria also produces many herbs used medicinally in pharmacy.

FLORA AND FAUNA

Domestic animals of most kinds do well in Bulgaria, and in forests and mountains, bears, wolves, boars, jackals, foxes, mountain cats and wild goats are still found, and otters in the rivers. Wild birds range from geese, ducks and buzzards to pheasants and black game, and among birds of prey are eagles and vultures. The rivers contain salmon, sterlet (a kind of sturgeon), mountain trout and carp, while mackerel and turbot are prolific in the Black Sea.

Five centuries of Muslim rule were bound to leave their mark on the Bulgarian character and way of life, yet there is a strong thread of con-tinuity linking modern with medieval Bulgaria. A number of towns

NATIONAL CHARACTER-ISTICS

19

bear Turkish names – for instance, Kazanluk and Pazarjik – while others, such as Chirpan and Shumen, retain a large Turkish population element. The Tomboul mosque in Shumen is one of the finest in the Balkan peninsula. One may still see Tatar and Turkish women walking about the streets of Bulgarian towns in their brightly coloured trousers gathered at the ankle. The Bulgarian, moreover, will signify assent in Turkish fashion, by shaking his head, the contrary by nodding.

The Bulgarian Christian population is a mixed one; their physical appearance takes several forms. For the most part, Bulgarians are sturdy and compact in build, often with dark hair and tanned complexion, though brunettes and blondes are not uncommon. Many of the men are handsome in a Mediterranean way, and beautiful women of Thracian character are frequently seen alongside the more stolid peasant types.

Less volatile and flamboyant than their neighbours the Serbs, the Romanians and the Greeks, the Bulgarians are industrious, tolerant and hospitable; but they are dogged fighters in what they regard as a just cause. In the main they possess a well-developed artistic sense which tends towards the picturesque. This is evinced by the painted houses of Plovdiv, Tărnovo and Koprivshtitsa, also by the national costume, featuring embroidered shirts and bodices and richly coloured skirts for the women, and baggy trousers and high boots for the men.

Plate 62,
Fig. 42

Bulgarians have long been renowned as singers and minstrels. Today, their basses are sought after by international opera houses, and their choirs compete with success in the Welsh national Eisteddfod. The Bulgarian choral ensemble and musical round dance have their roots in ancient times, being portrayed in medieval frescoes and manuscript illuminations.

Though far from superstitious, the Bulgarians regard Orthodox Christianity as a valuable ingredient of their way of life. The auto-cephalous national Church, which traces its descent from Saints Cyril and Methodius, has its own Patriarch; it played a leading role in the nineteenth-century freedom movement.

CHAPTER II

Bulgarian Origins : Early Settlers and Invaders

Bulgaria occupies a strategic position at the junction of ancient migration routes leading from Central Europe and South Russia towards Greece and the Sea of Marmara, and in the reverse direction. Climatically and geographically, the Balkans were excellently suited to the needs of primitive man, so that the area has been inhabited since Palaeolithic times, and yields up remains from the Abbevillian culture onwards.

The Thracian plain was famed for its dense population and advanced culture during the Bronze Age and in Hellenistic times. The Thracians, as we see from their beautiful vases, and from the murals on the Kazanluk tomb, were a graceful long-skulled, dark-haired and aristocratic race, though much diluted by Roman colonization and immigration from Asia Minor, Greece and Syria.

THE THRACIANS
Plates 2, 3

Relations with Greece and the Greek people have long played a role in the evolution of culture, art and commerce on the territory of present-day Bulgaria. Colonists from Miletus brought trade and advanced industrial crafts and artistic techniques to the Black Sea coastal region from the seventh century BC onwards; in ports such as Nessebăr, Greek is still spoken today by ordinary people in the street, as the writer noticed in 1971. The fact that Thrace was drawn into the orbit of Hellenistic culture must be counted a great benefit in the history of civilization on the Balkan peninsula.

THE GREEKS

Plates 30-32

Christian Byzantium also brought the people many advantages, even though good administration had to be paid for by burdensome taxes and levies. However, the Byzantines failed to protect the territory against successive waves of barbarian invasions, until most of the Balkan region was lost to the realm of Christian Byzantium during the sixth century AD. But later, in the ninth century, there came from that quarter the legacy of Cyril and Methodius, with all that this implied in the field of literature, art and Christian philosophy. During Ottoman times, how, ever, a less happy relationship developed; the Phanariot Greek clergy became associated with forces which aimed at rooting out Bulgaria's distinctive Slavonic culture, and merging the people into a common Ottoman pattern dictated from Istanbul.

THE ROMANS Not to be underestimated is the legacy of Rome in the Balkans. From the time of Augustus (63 BC–AD 14), the territory of present-day Bulgaria was an integral part of the Roman Empire. Two provinces were formed from the region: Thrace and Moesia. The latter province took in the territory of the main Balkan range and lands north of it, as far as the Danube. Originally a single province, under an imperial legate (who probably also had control of Achaea and Macedonia), it was divided by Domitian into Upper and Lower Moesia, the western and eastern portions respectively, separated by the river Cebrus.

Being a frontier province, Moesia was protected by stations and castles erected along the right bank of the Danube, while a wall was built from Axiopolis to Tomi (Constanza) as a protection against Scythian and Sarmatian incursions. When Aurelian was forced to abandon Dacia (modern Romania) to the barbarians between AD 270 and 275, many of the inhabitants were resettled south of the Danube, and the central portion of Moesia took the name of Dacia Aureliani.

Numerous archaeological remains testify to the advanced level of life in Moesia under the Roman Empire. The country was furnished with a whole network of roads linked to the Via Traiana, which connected Byzantium with Rome. The modern capital of Sofia, then named Ulpia Serdica, was already a fine town with a city wall, a portion of which still stands. The ruins of Nicopolis ad Istrum (Nikiup), a few miles north of Tărnovo, give us a good idea of the excellent urban planning which characterized even small provincial towns in Moesia at this period. At the port of Varna (Odessos), the colossal Roman baths rival in scale and conception the Baths of Caracalla in Rome, while the hinterland was dotted with comfortable Roman villas, of which that at Madara is a well-known example.

Roman Thrace also attained to a high level of civilization. Apart from the ancient Black Sea ports of Mesembria (Nessebăr), Anchialos

(Pomorie) and Apollonia (Sozopol), the main Roman show-place was Trimontium, the former city of Philippopolis, the modern Plovdiv. First incorporated into the Roman Empire by Claudius, the city was provided with a great encircling rampart by Marcus Aurelius, and is referred to by contemporaries as the most brilliant metropolis in the province of Thrace. The Greek satirist Lucian (AD 125–92) has a passage describing Trimontium as 'the biggest and most beautiful of all towns', and devotes several lines of an imaginary dialogue between Heracles and Hermes to dilating on the scenic attractions of the Thracian plain and the Balkan range in the background.

The Goths invaded Moesia and Thrace in AD 250, and occupied   THE GOTHS
Trimontium for some twenty years before being repulsed by the emperor Aurelian. Hard pressed from the north by the Huns, the Goths again crossed the Danube in AD 376, in the reign of Valens, who gave them asylum and permitted them to settle in Moesia. But dissension soon broke out between the Goths and the Romans. Aided by powerful contingents of Huns, Alans and Sarmatians, the Gothic leader Fritigern defeated and slew the emperor Valens in a great battle near Adrianople (AD 378). These Goths, who settled permanently in the territory of Bulgaria, are known as Moeso-Goths, and it was for them that Bishop Ulfilas (311–83) translated the Bible into Gothic. It is interesting to note that Ulfilas lived and worked for many years near the site of the medieval city of Great Tărnovo.   *Fig. 16*

This fact serves to emphasize that the history of the Balkans as an   EARLY
important centre of Christianity dates back at least as far as the fourth   CHRISTIAN-
century. Bulgaria was a Christian land, in large part, at the time of   ITY
Constantine the Great. This fact is sometimes understressed by Slavonic historians, who place the main emphasis on the much later conversion of the Slavs and Bulgars, in the ninth century, by Cyril and Methodius and their disciples. It is worth recalling that in AD 342 an important Church council took place in Serdica (Sofia), attended by 170 bishops, including St Athanasius the Great; John Cassian (360–435), the first Abbot of Marseilles, came from the Dobrudja.

The struggle between Rome and Constantinople for ecclesiastical jurisdiction in this area began as early as the fifth century, and the Council of Chalcedon (AD 451) already had to discuss the question as to who had the right to consecrate the Metropolitans of Thrace. Early Byzantine churches, in a ruined state, are abundant in Thrace and in northeastern Bulgaria. The land became pagan again as a result of the Slav and proto-Bulgar incursions of the sixth to eighth centuries. Thus, in regard to the Balkan region, the missions of Cyril and Methodius and their followers may be seen as the re-conversion of an area which had long before been an integral part of early Christendom.

THE HUNS

The fifth and sixth centuries witnessed the gradual breakdown of settled urban life in Bulgarian territory. The Huns, Getae, Gepids and Avars wrought havoc in the land. During the Hunnic invasions of AD 441–47, the church of St Sophia in Serdica (Sofia) was destroyed for what appears to have been the fourth time since its foundation.

Plate 17

Before the Byzantine Empire had shaken off the terror of the Goths and the Huns, new tribes of barbarians appeared on its Balkan frontiers. Under Emperor Justin I (518–27) the Antae began to constitute a menace to the empire. These Antae belonged to a Slavic ethnic group known to the Ancients as the Wends, who inhabited an area between the rivers Oder and Dnieper.

THE SLAVS

Emperor Justinian (527–65) was faced with massive incursions by the Slavs themselves, which he sought to counteract by erecting a strong inner chain of forts behind the lines of defence on the Danube. But these fortifications proved ineffectual, in the absence of sufficient troops to man them. The Slavs poured over the entire Balkan peninsula as far as the Adriatic, the Gulf of Corinth in Greece, and the shores of the Aegean, ravaging the heartland of the Byzantine Empire just at the time when Justinian's captains Belisarius and Narses were celebrating a series of brilliant but rather futile victories in Italy and the western Mediterranean.

At first the invading hordes, which numbered contingents of proto-Bulgar tribes among their ranks, were content to plunder the towns and countryside, and then retreat north of the Danube with their booty. But within a few decades, civilized town life became impossible over much of the Balkan region. In Bulgaria, such key Roman centres as Transmariscus, Kaliakra, Abrittus and Marcianopolis soon ceased to exist.

By the accession of Emperor Heraclius in 610, seafaring Slavs were

even making landings in Crete. The capital of Dalmatia, Salona, fell to
the Slavs in 614, about which time they also seized and ravaged Singi/
dunum (Belgrade), Naissus (Nish) and Serdica (Sofia), the early Slav
name of which is Sredets. The Byzantines managed to hold on to their
ports on the Adriatic and Black Sea coasts, but the hinterland of the
Balkan peninsula is from now on referred to in the Greek sources as
'Sclavinia'.

One of the main invasion routes through Bulgaria was the Struma
valley. On no less than four occasions (AD 586, 609, 620 and 622) Slavs
and Avars advanced down this valley to lay siege to Thessalonica, but
always in vain – their defeat being popularly attributed to the interven/
tion of St Demetrius. In 626, a force of Slavs, Avars and proto/Bulgars
besieged Constantinople itself, but without success. Nevertheless, for
some two centuries, the whole of Greece was dominated by the Slav
invaders, to such an extent that two thousand place/names in that
country have been identified by Professor Max Vasmer as being of
Slavonic origin.

Fig. 3

These events had profound repercussions on the ethnic composition
of the Balkan peninsula, in particular that of Bulgaria. A large propor/
tion of the ancient population – Thracians, Illyrians, Greeks, Roman
colonists – were slaughtered or led away into captivity, or else conquered
and assimilated. Some of the ancient Thracians, driven up into in/
accessible mountains, helped to form the nucleus of the Vlach (Walla/
chian) element in Bulgaria and Romania in medieval times. The Byzan/
tines attempted to remedy this problem by resettling affected areas with
fresh colonists, including Goths, Sarmatians, Bastarnae (an eastern
offshoot of the Germanic family of peoples), Carpi (a Dacian tribe,
established in Pannonia and Moesia), and even some of the Heruli (a
people who are supposed to have originated in Denmark, and later
founded a powerful kingdom at the mouth of the Elbe). This policy was
only partially successful, because the Slav invaders became more and
more numerous, and began to settle down permanently on Bulgarian
territory over a wide area.

While some areas west of the Yantra retained much of their old
Thracian population, we can trace the influx of the Slavs in northeastern
Bulgaria by the general substitution of Slavonic place/names for Thracian
and Greek ones: thus, Odessos is replaced by Varna, Dionysopolis

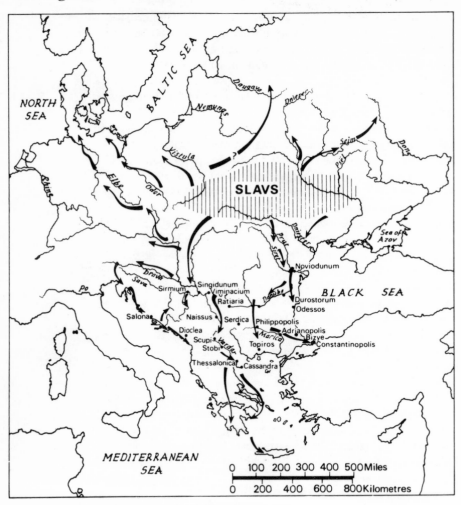

Fig. 3 Slavonic expansion to and colonization of the Balkan Peninsula, central and northern Europe, during the sixth and seventh centuries AD. The Slavonic homeland area is shown by vertical hatching; the towns are those of the Byzantine Empire. (After Gimbutas)

by Balchik, Marcianopolis by Devnya, Provaton (Provadia) by Ovech. The Thracian language swiftly died out, the latest mention of a Thracian name occurring in the pages of the Byzantine chronicler Theophanes, who wrote around AD 810. At the same time, a number of Thracian place-names were taken over by the Slavs, though in modified form. Thus Pulpudeva, the Thracian name for Philippopolis (modern Plovdiv) was turned into Pludin, then Plăvdiv; the river Yatrus was transformed into the Yantra; the river Timacus becomes Timok; the river Almus, Lom; the river Utus, Vit; the river Nestos, Mesta; the Rhodope Mountains, Rodopa.

Many Thracian survivals have been detected in the sphere of Bulgarian national costume and folk tradition. It is thought that the Bulgarian *yamurluk*, the hooded felt cloak worn by shepherds, as well as the characteristic medieval pointed cap or bonnet, have Thracian origins. The same can be said of the cult of the Thracian horseman, which crops up from time to time among the early Bulgarians. Also of Thracian origin are the performances of mummers known as *kukeri*, who carry out rites connected with the spring-time fertility cult. These *kukeri* all wear fantastic masks and a large number of bells round the waist. Again, there is the ceremonial pruning of the vine-shoots on February 14, the feast of St Trifon Zarezan, patron saint of vineyards, who is the Christian embodiment of Dionysus, just as the Slav god Perun passed into the Orthodox Calendar as St Ilia, on which occasion wine is poured formally on the earth. Another interesting old custom is the ritual fire dance, known as 'nestinarstvo', performed on June 2 and 3, the days of Saints Constantine and Helena. Specially characteristic of the Strandzha district, this is a pagan custom which later acquired overtones of Christianity: women dance on hot coals with bare feet, but somehow manage to remain unscathed.

Plate 61

The ancient Thracians, along with remnants of the Roman settlers or 'provincials', played a significant role in the formation of the Vlach or Wallachian people, who make up a substantial nucleus of the modern Romanian nation. From the tenth century onwards, we hear of survivors of the old Romanized Thracian and Illyrian tribes, called Aromani or else Vlachoi, leading a nomadic life as herdsmen in parts of the Balkan range, as well as in Thessaly, Thrace, Macedonia and Serbia, also north

THE VLACHS

of the Danube, in the Carpathians. The first mention of Vlachs in Byzantine historical sources occurs about the year 976 when, according to the *Chronicle* of Cedrenus (ii. 439), a brother of the Bulgarian tsar Samuel was murdered by 'certain Vlach footpads' at a spot called Fair Oaks, between Castoria and Prespa.

Originally dwelling predominantly south of the Danube, the Vlachs played an important role in the Second Bulgarian Empire, officially styled the Empire of the Bulgarians and the Vlachs. Later, their principal habitat shifted north of the Danube. The end of the twelfth century found the Vlachs taking possession of the fertile plains and fields of Romania, to become settled farmers in the manner of their Thracian forefathers. This trend was encouraged by the disappearance of the old Slav population of Romania, decimated by invading hordes of Magyars, Pechenegs, Alans and Cumans.

THE SEVEN TRIBES   Within Bulgaria itself, particularly the northern hill country, the round-headed, fair or red-haired Slavs were for long the dominant ethnic element. From about AD 600, the confederation of the Seven Tribes controlled the area from the Yantra to the Black Sea. .

These ancient Slavs were expert farmers and stock-breeders. They were also renowned as carpenters, iron-founders and blacksmiths. They were strong and vigorous, and able to withstand physical hardship. Contemporaries commented that if only they had been able to unite among themselves, no state could have resisted them. However, they preferred to retain their primitive and democratic clan system, only electing a prince (*knyaz, arkhont*) in time of war or national emergency. Accounts differ as to their character: some authors describe them as cruel, liable to impale or otherwise slaughter any unwanted captives. Others describe the Slavs as amiable, and even ready to make friends with their former prisoners of war. According to the *Strategicum* of the writer known as the Pseudo-Maurice:

> They do not keep their prisoners in captivity for an indefinite period, as do the other tribes, but they assign a fixed time limit, and leave them the freedom to decide whether they would rather return to their homeland on payment of a ransom, or else remain with them as free men and friends.

The same authority adds that the Slavs were friendly towards strangers, and escorted them with care from one place to another, when they required travel facilities. Conviviality was encouraged by copious imbibing of mead, which the Slavs brewed from honey.

There exists a Persian geographical treatise called *Ḥudūd al-ʿĀlam* or 'Regions of the World', written in AD 982, which gives an illuminating insight into the way of life of the Slavs, as well as that of other peoples of the Near East and Russian regions. The anonymous Persian geographer has a special discourse (Chapter 43) on the Slavs or *Ṣaqāliba*. In the translation by the late Professor Vladimir Minorsky, we read:

> The people live among the trees and sow nothing except millet. They have no grapes but possess plenty of honey from which they prepare wine [i.e., mead] and the like. Their vessels [casks] for wine are made of wood, and there are people who annually prepare a hundred of such vessels of wine. They possess herds of swine which are just like herds of sheep. They burn the dead. When a man dies, his wife, if she loves him, kills herself. They all wear shirts, and shoes over the ankles. All of them are fire-worshippers. They possess stringed instruments unknown in the Islamic countries, on which they play. Their arms are shields, javelins, and lances. . . . They spend the winter in huts and underground dwellings. They possess numer-ous castles and fortresses. They dress mostly in linen stuffs. They think it their religious duty to serve the king. They possess two towns.

Plate 62

Our learned Persian is apparently wrong in thinking that the ancient Slavs were fire-worshippers, though there is evidence of a cult of the sun. Their chief deity was the Thunderer Perun, with whom was associated Svarog, god of heaven. Other senior gods were Dazhbog, god of fertility, Khors, the solar deity, and Veles or Volos, god of cattle and stockbreeding. A hostile deity was Stribog, god of storms. The Slavs also worshipped many subsidiary gods and goddesses, and believed in spirits, nymphs and water sprites (*rusalkas* and *samodivas*), who inhabited caves, rivers and forests, and to whom they offered sacrifices and gifts.

We learn from the sixth-century historian Procopius that the Balkan Slavs in his time were already in the habit of sacrificing animals to their deity Perun. The cock was a frequent sacrificial victim; a bull, bear or

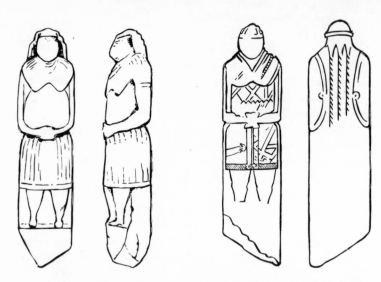

Fig. 4 Pagan Slavonic female idols, or 'Kamennye Baby', found at Indjeköy (Zlatna niva), near Shumen, and now in the Shumen Museum. Stone. Average height 2½ metres; the base sunk into the ground approx. 70 cm. (After Naslednikova)

he-goat was slain only on great festival occasions. The animal slaughtered was considered to be imbued with the holy manna of his patron god, made manifest in the animal's living body. When the animal was killed and eaten communally, the group as a whole would be strength-ened. Such beliefs have persisted in Russia, the Balkans, and also in Georgia and Armenia, throughout the Christian era and right up to modern times.

Fig. 4

The worship of fertility and the 'Mother Goddess' is evinced among the ancient Slavs by the cult of the so-called '*Kamennye Baby*', which are great female images carved in stone, and replete with the symbolism of human reproduction. A fine group may be seen in Bulgaria at the Shumen Museum.

Although they were driven by the Slavs from most of the Balkan peninsula, the demoralized Byzantines were saved from complete disaster by the Slavs' innate dislike of anything that smacked of perman-ent military or political authority. Thus, the Greeks were able during the seventh century to keep some measure of hegemony over certain coastal areas. Once the threatened advance of Islam could be checked in the East, there seemed to be every prospect of a rapid reconquest of the region which we know as Bulgaria. This prospect was nullified by the arrival south of the Danube of the warlike and well-organized followers of Khan Asparukh, founder of the medieval Slavo-Bulgarian realm. These proto-Bulgars, perhaps no more than fifty thousand strong to begin with, soon distinguished themselves by their excellent organiza- tion, warlike energy, and centralized military bureaucracy; they came to play a role in Balkan history comparable to that of the Indo-European Hittites in ancient Anatolia, the Varangians in early Rus', and the Normans in England following the conquest of 1066.

The renown of the Bulgars had reached Europe and the Near East THE BULGARS long before they arrived in the Balkans. One early reference occurs in a Latin chronicle, dating from the year 354, which mentions among the offspring of Shem a certain 'Ziezi ex quo Vulgares' – though admittedly Theodore Mommsen, who studied this chronicle in 1850, was of the opinion that this phrase might possibly be a later interpolation made about the year 539. There are also early references to Bulgars in Armenia, contained in the Armenian history attributed to Moses of Khorene (eighth–ninth centuries). Here we read of a Bulgar tribe headed by Vkhundur Vund settling in the Basean district of Armenia during the reign of King Valarshak, towards the end of the fourth century AD; in the view of Moses of Khorene, the Bulgar leader gave his name to this region, known today as Vanand. Another passage from Moses of Khorene tells of tribal trouble in the North Caucasian region, as a result of which many Bulgars broke loose from their associate tribes and migrated to fertile regions south of Kogh. This event is assigned to the reign of Arshak, son of Valarshak.

Additional references to Bulgars occur in the anonymous Armenian geographic work of the seventh century, often attributed to Anania Shirakatsi. This authority was well informed on the lands of the Turks and Bulgars, which stretched far afield from the north side of Nikopsis, on the Black Sea coast. The Armenian geographer states that the principal tribes of Bulgars were called Kuphi-Bulgars, Duchi-Bulgars, Oghkhundur-Bulgars, and Kidar-Bulgars, by the last-named of which he meant the Kidarites, a branch of the Huns.

The ethnicon 'Bulgar' is of Old Turkic origin – from the word *bulgha*, 'to mix'. This derivation serves to underline the complex racial make-up of the proto-Bulgars, who were more of a tribal federation than a specific tribe. The linguistic and archaeological evidence leads us to conclude that the proto-Bulgars were a hybrid people, in which a Central Asian Turkic or Mongol core was combined with Iranian, and notably Alanic or Sarmatian elements.

The proto-Bulgars spoke an ancient Turkic language, of which about twenty words are embedded in the Greek texts of the proto-Bulgarian inscriptions, over eighty in number, found in the territory of the Balkan Bulgars, and dating from the eighth and ninth centuries. The physical type was largely Mongoloid or Altaic. These ancient Bulgars had squarish faces, with protruding cheek bones and slanting eyes, and they were short and stocky. They shaved their heads, leaving some hair on the top, which they wore in a pigtail. They were clad in long fur coats in winter, belted at the waist. Their headgear was a cone-shaped cap edged with fur, and they wore soft boots on their feet. Some of them bound bands around the heads of their children in infancy, in an attempt to produce an elongated cranium, which was much admired. The women, who were for the most part veiled, wore wide breeches and had body sashes with ornaments of iron, copper, glass and bone.

Fig. 5

The main peace-time activity of the proto-Bulgars was stockbreeding. They chiefly raised horses, and the tail of a horse was used as a banner in battle. Whereas the Slavs cultivated corn and other crops for their own consumption, the Bulgars mostly ate meat, including horsemeat, and also curdled milk. They worshipped various animals, each tribe having its own totem, and their calendar was based on the 'animal cycle'

Fig. 5 Proto-Bulgar cavalryman with ceremonial lance, confronting a foot-soldier. Graffito on a stone block from Preslav fortress, about AD 900. (After Hensel)

system. Their chief deity, however, was the immortal Tangra or Tengri, creator of the world. They also worshipped the sun, moon and stars, and some tribes had idols of silver and bronze.

The ruling khan or khaqan was regarded as a religious leader, with semi-divine attributes. Though his rule tended towards absolute power, an element of democracy was provided by the council of six chief *boïlyas* or *bolyars*. Army generals bore the title of *baghain*. There was a category of high dignitary at court, known as *sampsis*, a title connected with the Turkish word *san*, 'dignity' or 'esteem', a word also encountered later in Russian with the same significance.

The judge and public executioner was called the *qanar tikin*, from two Turkish words meaning 'blood-spilling' and 'young hero' respectively. There was a special class of citizen known as *tarkhan*; these were privileged freemen, exempt from taxes. Later on, around AD 950, we find mention of an official termed *chărgoboïlya*, or head of state security; the post was once held by a certain Mostich, whose tombstone has been preserved.

Fig. 9

The ancient Bulgar army was dominated by its fast-moving cavalry, and by the fifth century was regarded with fear in Central Europe. According to the historian Paulus Diaconus (*c.* 720–800), Bulgar forces assailed the army of Agelmund, first of the Lombard kings. The Bulgars slew Agelmund and kidnapped his only daughter, but were finally routed by the new Lombard king, Lamissio.

THE BULGAR
ARMY

At that time the Bulgars became involved in the migrations of the Huns and other eastern nomads, which caused havoc not only in Central but in Western Europe as well. It is often argued that the semi-legendary founder of the Bulgar nation, Avitokhol, was in fact none other than the famous Attila (d. 453). This Avitokhol is the first ruler to occur in the 'List of Bulgar Princes' discovered in Russia in a medieval Slavonic manuscript, and providing a vital key to early Bulgarian chronology.

However this may be, the ancient Bulgars were already featuring in the annals of Byzantium before the end of the fifth century. They are regularly linked in the sources with the Utigurs, whose name comes from Old Turkish *utighur*, meaning 'an allied people'; likewise with the Onogurs, whose name, also Old Turkish, signifies 'the ten confederate tribes', the Turkic form being *On-uyghur*. Prominent too were the Kutrigurs, a name deriving from Old Turkish *kötrügür*, meaning 'conspicuous', 'eminent' or 'renowned'. The Greeks do not always distinguish accurately between these various tribal names, sometimes using them when actually the Bulgars are meant.

In the year 481, the emperor Zeno employed Bulgar mercenaries against the Ostrogoth king Theodoric the Great (454–526), when he attacked Constantinople. Bulgars also fought against another barbarian leader named Theodoric, son of Triarius, who attacked the city in 487. By now, some Bulgars were already settled north of the lower Danube, in the territory of modern Romania.

A little later, in 488, Theodoric the Great invaded Italy, and on the way fought a bloody engagement against an army of Bulgars and Gepids near Sirmium. The Bulgar commander, Buzan, fell in battle. Theodoric himself killed a Bulgar chief named Libertem (probably Turkic *Alb-ertem*, meaning 'heroic virtue'). The Latin rhetorician and poet Ennodius (474–521), who was bishop of Pavia, refers to the 'indomita Bulgarum juventus', while Cassiodorus (487–583), who served as Latin secretary to Theodoric the Great, speaks in one of his works of 'Bulgari toto orbe terribiles'.

During the reign of the emperor Anastasius (491–518), the Bulgars made several incursions into Thrace and Illyricum. Bulgars were found in the forces of the insurgent leader Vitalian, who was a renegade Byzantine commander-in-chief in Thrace. Vitalian, with his Bulgars and other troops, aided by a fleet, advanced three times right up to the massive 'Long Wall' of Constantinople, before being beaten off decisively by the loyalists. In 539, the Bulgars overran the Dobrudja, Moesia and the Balkan region, as far as Thrace. The sixth-century Byzantine writer Jordanes (himself ethnically an Alan or a Goth) complains in AD 551 of 'instantia quotidiana Bulgarorum, Antarum et Sclavinorum', though elsewhere he gives credit to the Bulgars for intro-ducing grey Siberian squirrel fur into the orbit of international trade.

In 545, Emperor Justinian offered the Antae a large sum of money, lands on the left bank of the Danube, and the status of imperial *foederati*, on condition that they guarded the river against the Bulgars. Some of the Kutrigurs, however, were allowed to settle in Thrace, in spite of which they and their confederates staged a great invasion of the Balkans and

Greece in the year 559. The noble Belisarius had to be called in to defend the Empire from imminent peril.

Among many other warlike episodes involving the ancient Bulgars, we may cite the events of the year 568, when hordes of them surged into Italy from Central Europe, under the leadership of the Lombard king Alboin. The following year, Boyan, khaqan of the Avars, sent ten thousand Bulgars and Kutrigurs against the Romans in Dalmatia, where they destroyed forty Roman castles. In 596, the Byzantine general Petros suffered defeat at Anasamus on the Danube at the hands of a force of six thousand Bulgars.

Further migrations of Bulgars into Italy took place around 630. Driven out of Bavaria by Dagobert I, king of the Franks (629–39), some seven hundred Bulgars under a prince named Altsek took refuge in the duchy of Benevento and were granted lands in the Abruzzi by Duke Grimoald. The historian Paulus Diaconus records in the following century that these Bulgars were now speaking Latin, though they still remembered their old Turkic tongue.

During the sixth century, an important state called 'Old Great Bulgaria' grew up, extending over the North Caucasian steppe, the Kuban, and large areas of what is now the Ukraine. The capital of this new state was at Phanagoria, the modern Taman, on the sea of Azov. Such Byzantine historians as Theophanes (752–818), author of the *Chronography*, and Nicephorus (750–829), regarded Old Great Bulgaria as an ancient and long-established power. Indeed, by the time that these authorities lived and wrote, Old Great Bulgaria had already been largely submerged by the rising power of the Khazars.

OLD GREAT BULGARIA

Byzantium took great interest in the development of Old Great Bulgaria and other semi-barbarian powers in the northern Black Sea region. The historian Zacharias Scholasticus, who was bishop of Mitylene from 536 to 553, refers to Christian missions going from the Byzantine Empire to try to convert the Bulgars and Huns north of the Caucasus. A Hunnic prince named Grod had proceeded to Constantinople in 528 and adopted Christianity. On his return home to the Crimea, Grod melted down the pagan idols made of silver and electrum, and used them in ingot form as currency. The Huns of the Crimea soon rose in revolt against this sacrilege, assassinated Grod, and replaced him as their leader by his brother Mugel. Despite these misadventures, however, trade, diplomatic and religious contacts between Constantinople and the Crimean Huns and Old Bulgaria continued to develop on a regular basis.

During the late sixth and early seventh centuries, Old Bulgaria fell under the sway of the Western Turkish or Türküt khaqanate. This gave rise to several rebellions, in which many Bulgars lost their lives.

The zenith of the political might of Old Great Bulgaria is associated with the name of Khan Kubrat, who reigned for half a century up till his death about the year 642. There exists a tradition – disputed by Sir Steven Runciman – that Kubrat was brought up and educated in Byzantium, possibly as a hostage, as was a common practice in those days. However this may be, a Bulgar prince, presumably Kubrat, came on an embassy to Constantinople in 619. (Some authorities consider that this prince was Organa, Kubrat's uncle.) The potentate in question was greeted with great honours by the emperor Heraclius, granted the imperial title of Patrician, baptized as a Christian, and sent back to his homeland as a friend and ally of the Byzantine State.

By 635, Kubrat had united under his rule virtually all the Bulgar and Hunnic tribes living in the region of the Sea of Azov and North Caucasia, and shaken off the yoke of the West Turkish or Türküt khaqan, who previously exercized supreme hegemony over the region. A contemporary of the last Sasanian Great King, Yazdgard III (632–51), Kubrat maintained political and cultural links with Iran. These links were to bring forth artistic fruits after the Bulgars had long since moved into the Balkans (see Chapter VII); the Madara Horseman is, for example, in the great tradition of Naqsh-i-Rustam and Bishapur, and the Bulgar Sublime Khan's dining hall equipped with gold and silverware recalls the finest Sasanian examples. Not to be underestimated either is the extent of Kubrat's commercial and diplomatic exchanges with the great cities of Khwarazm and Sogdiana in Central Asia, then at the height of their efflorescence.

Kubrat's realm broke up after his death. According to the Byzantine chroniclers Theophanes and Nicephorus, he left a will bidding his five sons remain together in unity and mutual solidarity; but they soon went their several ways, thus precipitating the break-up of Old Great Bulgaria. The eldest, Baian or Batbaian, remained in Old Bulgaria. The second,

Plates 4, 5

Plates 12–16

Kotrag, crossed the Don and dwelt on the far side. The third, Asparukh, traversed the Dnieper with his followers and temporarily set up his encampment between that river and the Danube. The fourth son of Kubrat crossed the Carpathians and reached Pannonia, where he placed himself under the suzerainty of the Avar khaqan. The fifth travelled the farthest of all, arriving with his tribe in Italy, near Ravenna, where he made submission to the Byzantine emperor.

It should be added that the break-up of Old Bulgaria was further precipitated by the onslaught of the new power of the Khazars, who later adopted Judaism, and became the dominant power in the Eurasian steppes. The name of Kotrag, assigned by the Byzantine sources to Kubrat's second son, evidently represents the tribal name of the Kutri-gurs, who must have reasserted their autonomy once Kubrat's powerful hand was removed by death. Where the fourth and fifth sons of Kubrat are concerned, it seems doubtful whether in fact Bulgars were still moving westwards from the Azov region into Pannonia and Italy as late as the mid-seventh century. However, they were active there some-what earlier, from the time of Attila the Hun. Possibly the accounts of Theophanes and Nicephorus are partly symbolic in character, and incorporate memories of earlier Bulgar incursions into the Frankish and Lombard territories, as already briefly related.

Of prime importance for our present study are the exploits of Kubrat's third son, Asparukh, the one who set off towards the Danube, and ultimately became the veritable founder of the Slavo-Bulgar state in the Balkans. It is interesting to find the Armenian seventh-century geo-grapher, usually identified as Anania Shirakatsi, noting:

> In Thrace there are two mountains and rivers, one of which is the Danube, which divides up into six arms, and forms a lake and an island called Pyuki [Pevka]. On this island lives Aspar-Khruk, son of Kubraat, who fled away before the Khazars, from the Bulgarian hills, and pursued the Avars towards the west. He has settled down in this spot . . .

As for the Bulgars who stayed behind in what is now southeastern Russia and the Ukraine, we may distinguish particularly those of 'Inner Bulgaria', between the Don and the Dnieper, and the separate and distinct community of the Muslim Bulgars or Bulghars, centred on the great trading city of Bulghar on the Volga. In the tenth century, Russian and Byzantine sources begin to mention a people known as 'Black Bulgarians', neighbours of the Khazars, and evidently occupying part of the territory known earlier as Inner Bulgaria. The Nikon Chronicle and other Russian sources further refer to colonies of Bulghars living as far north as the river Kama. The modern Chuvash people, also the Kazan Tatars, owe much ethnically and culturally to earlier Bulgar communities dwelling along the rivers Volga and Kama. Thus we may trace a continuous thread running through many centuries of Russian history, and linking Old Great Bulgaria with communities still extant in the Soviet Union today.

THE
ARMENIANS

Another ethnic element which makes its appearance in Thrace and the Balkan region during early Byzantine times is that of the Armenians, whose original homeland was in eastern Anatolia and the Ararat district of Transcaucasia. Initially, the Armenians were resettled in Thrace as part of a deliberate Byzantine policy of 'divide and rule'. Emperor Justinian (527–65) began by transporting a number of Armenian families to Thrace. A transplantation on a vaster scale was conceived by Emperor Maurice (582–602), and partially carried out.

The religious ferment in Armenia which in the seventh century gave rise to the Paulician heresy (see Chapter V) had the effect of bringing still more Armenians into the Byzantine Empire. During the reign of Constantine V Copronymus (740–75), thousands of Armenians and Monophysite Syrians were gathered by the Byzantine armies during their raids in the regions of Marash, Melitene and Erzerum, and mostly settled in Thrace. Similar transfers of population took place under Emperor Leo IV (775–80). Many of these colonists who had settled in Thrace were seized by the ferocious Khan Krum of Bulgaria (803–14), and carried away into northern Bulgaria and across the Danube. According to tradition, the parents of the future Byzantine emperor Basil I, and the infant Basil himself, were among these prisoners.

The Armenian groups already settled in Byzantine Thrace were constantly reinforced by later arrivals. During the tenth century, in the reign of John Tzimiskes (himself an Armenian), a considerable number of Paulician schismatics were removed from the frontier regions of

Anatolia and settled in and around Plovdiv (Philippopolis). These Paulicians were predominantly Armenians, though they included Anatolian and Cappadocian elements. Around the year 988, Armenians were settled also in Macedonia, brought there by Basil II (known as the 'Bulgar-slayer') to serve as a bulwark against the Bulgarians, and also to increase the country's commercial prosperity.

The Armenian Paulicians have given their name to the important town of Pavlikeni, in northern Bulgaria, not far from Great Tărnovo. They played a key role in propagating the Bogomil heresy (see Chapter V) in Bulgaria and the Balkans, also in Byzantium generally.

It is also worth noting that one of the last and most valiant rulers of the First Bulgarian Empire, King Samuel, had an Armenian mother named Hripsimé; his brothers bore the biblical names David, Moses and Aaron, common among Armenians. According to the Armenian historian Asoghik, Samuel and his family were natives of the Armenian province of Derjan, west of Erzerum. Samuel and his brother David began their career in the service of the Byzantines, and defected to the Bulgarian side during one of the Byzantine campaigns in the Balkans. Samuel's reign, which lasted from 993 until his death in 1014 (see Chapter III), is renowned as a saga of resistance to the might of Emperor Basil II Bulgaroktonos.

During the eleventh century, an important new people makes its appearance in South Russia and then in the Balkans and Central Europe, namely the Cumans or Polovtsians, immortalized by Borodin in his opera, *Prince Igor*. The Cumans came from Central Asia, and overthrew the remains of the old Khazar state on the Volga. After the defeat of the Pechenegs by Yaroslav of Kiev, the Cumans extended their dominion still further westwards, reaching the Dnieper in 1055. The early westward raids of the Cumans, as when they invaded Hungary in 1071 and Byzantine territory in 1086 and 1094, in alliance with the Pechenegs, were not made in force, and were repulsed.

THE CUMANS
OR
POLOVTSIANS

Early in the thirteenth century, the Cumans are found as allies of the Bulgarian tsar Kaloyan (1197–1207), whose wife was herself a Cuman. With Tsar Kaloyan's backing, the Cumans engaged in annual raids against the Latins who conquered Constantinople. The Bulgar-Cuman alliance had to be renewed annually, since at the approach of summer,

Fig. 12

the Cumans would invariably retire to their own steppes to enjoy their booty. A few decades later, the Mongol invasion of South Russia forced many of the Cumans to move permanently into the Balkans, as the proto-Bulgars had done six centuries previously. Large numbers of Cumans crossed the Danube in leather boats, and took refuge in Bulgaria, where they played a prominent military and political role right up to the Ottoman conquest in 1393. Another group of Cumans, numbering some two hundred thousand, took refuge in Hungary, where they adopted Christianity as the Magyars had done, and retained their ethnic and cultural individuality right up to the eighteenth century. The name by which the Hungarians know the Cumans is Kunok.

It is important to note that two of the later Bulgarian royal lines, the Terter and the Shishman dynasties, were partly of Cuman origin. The Cumans also produced a dynasty in Egypt, and intermarried with the kings and princes of Kiev, Serbia and Hungary.

Ethnically, the Cumans were akin to the Seljuq Turks. They were a talented and prolific race. They wore short kaftans and shaved their heads, except for two long plaits. Hunters and warriors, they left the cultivation of the soil to their subject tribes of Slavs. Russian sources, such as the Chronicle of Nestor, give an unfavourable account of them, alleging, for instance, that 'they love to shed blood, and boast that they eat carrion and the flesh of unclean beasts, such as the civet and the hamster; they marry their mothers-in-law and their daughters-in-law, and imitate in all things the example of their fathers.'

Their language has been preserved in the *Codex Cumanicus*, now in the library of St Mark's in Venice. This fourteenth-century manuscript contains an incomplete Cuman lexicon, a number of hymns, and a collection of riddles in Cuman. The language is clearly an East Turkic dialect. The community of the Gagauz – Turkish-speaking Orthodox Christians of northeast Bulgaria, the Dobrudja and Bessarabia – are said to be descendants of the Cumans. In Bulgaria, the Gagauz have been largely assimilated in recent times.

THE
PECHENEGS

For the sake of completeness, it is necessary to add a few words about the Pechenegs (or Patzinaks), who feature in Bulgarian history as allies of the Cumans, and spoke a related Turkic language. More uncouth and rapacious than the Cumans, the Pechenegs played a prominent part in

Balkan history after the destruction of Bulgarian independence by Emperor Basil II: between 1020 and 1030, they invaded Bulgaria from north of the Danube every year, and from 1048 to 1056 were continuously at war with Byzantium. At the close of these campaigns, the Byzantine government granted the Pechenegs lands for settlement within Bulgaria, but their depredations continued.

The Pechenegs still survive in Bulgaria, in the plain of Sofia, and are known as 'Sops'. The Oxford historian C. A. Macartney studied these Sops during the 1920s, and reported that they were despised by the other inhabitants of Bulgaria for their stupidity and bestiality, and dreaded for their savagery. 'They are a singularly repellent race, short-legged, yellow-skinned, with slanting eyes and projecting cheek-bones. Their villages are generally filthy, but the women's costumes show a barbaric profusion of gold lace.'

Such, then, were some of the elements, of highly disparate social background and cultural levels, which helped to make up the population of the First and Second Bulgarian Empires – both of them great powers of the Middle Ages. This population was formed in the main from a fusion of ancient autochtonous peoples from Thracian times, of Slavonic agriculturists, and of proto-Bulgars from the Eurasian steppes, the latter destined to fulfil in the Balkans their aspirations towards statehood and military conquest.

CHAPTER III
From Khanate to Imperium :
The First Bulgarian Empire

The well organized and massive immigrations of Khan Asparukh and his Bulgar followers from north to south of the Danube between the years 679 and 681 serve as a watershed in Bulgarian history. These dates have an importance comparable to that of the Norman invasion of 1066 in the history of the British Isles. A large and prosperous part of the Byzantine homeland, after being ravaged by the Slavs, was now systematically overrun and colonized by an alien race from the steppes, the proto-Bulgars. These proceeded to set up a military and political organization which was to challenge the supremacy, if not the very existence, of Constantinople itself.

The appearance of the proto-Bulgars under Asparukh at the mouth of the Danube was in itself no sudden or unexpected phenomenon. Asparukh himself was a scion of the illustrious house of Dulo, to which also belonged Attila the Hun. It is recorded by Shirakatsi that Asparukh and his followers were established on the Danube estuary at Pyuki (Pevka) from about AD 650. A quarter of a century later, the proto-Bulgars began to establish a bridgehead south of the estuary.

When the Byzantine government's efficient intelligence service brought early word of this development to Constantinople. Emperor Constantine IV Pogonatus (668–85) reacted vigorously. He hastened to conclude peace with the Arab caliph's invading Saracen forces, and rushed his armies to the Danube. In 680, a large squadron of Greek ships under the emperor's personal command sailed up the Black Sea coast, then disembarked north of the Danube delta. Byzantine cavalry squadrons were brought in from Anatolia, and reached the Danube via Thrace, only to get bogged down in the swampy marshes of the delta. The Bulgars evaded pitched battle with the Greeks; Emperor Constantine IV, stricken by illness, abandoned his forces and beat an ignominious retreat. The Byzantine army attempted to recross the Danube, but was routed by the Bulgars, who advanced as far as Varna.

A peace treaty was then signed, recognizing Khan Asparukh's annexation of the former Roman province of Moesia, and providing for the Byzantines to pay the Bulgars an annual tribute. The federation of the Seven Slav Tribes soon acknowledged the suzerainty of the Bulgars, and also paid tribute to Asparukh. The related Slav tribe of the Severi like-wise rendered homage to Asparukh, though they were exempted from paying tribute.

Khan Asparukh is credited with the foundation of Pliska, the original capital of the First Bulgarian Empire, situated on an undulating plain not far from the modern town of Shumen.

Plates 6–8

The exact numerical strength of the first Bulgar invasion horde is unknown, and may have been as little as fifty thousand. The role of these tough, well-disciplined steppe folk in galvanizing the scattered Slav agricultural communities into political and military activity was to prove crucial – comparable, in fact to the impact of Rurik and his Varangians on Kiev Rus' some two centuries later. It is true that the settled Slavs were ahead of the nomadic Bulgars in agriculture, weaving, and some of the arts of peace. On the other hand, it may be argued that the proto-Bulgars were in many respects in advance of the Slavs in stock-breeding, pottery, sculpture, and even monumental architecture. More-over, in literacy the Bulgars led the Slavs prior to the introduction of Christianity, and produced the remarkable corpus of proto-Bulgarian inscriptions – these were inscribed in Greek, though they contain over a score of proto-Bulgar terms, names, and titles.

Fig. 6

Historically speaking, the vital point is that the proto-Bulgars intro-duced into the chaotic Slav world of the Balkans the notion of an

Fig. 6 Wheel-turned Slavonic pottery from the settlement at Popina, northeastern Bulgaria. Eighth-ninth centuries AD. (After Gimbutas)

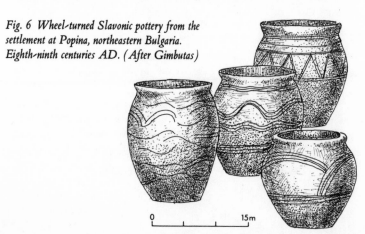

0   15m

imperial destiny, backed by a rigid military and social hierarchy. This hierarchy was controlled by a warlike central bureaucracy, answerable to a single chief, the Sublime Khan. The autocratic power of the khan was, however, kept in check by ancestral custom, as well as by the jealous rivalry of the clan chiefs or bolyars, who were often powerful enough to band together and dethrone or slay any khan who proved incompetent or otherwise unacceptable to this élite body. In those days of the survival of the fittest, the aggressive instincts of the proto-Bulgars and their well tried military aptitude provided a catalyst without which the creation of a viable Slav state in the Balkans would have been long delayed, if not permanently frustrated.

The precise character of the social and economic relations between the Balkan Slavs and the proto-Bulgars is hard to establish with precision. Byzantine chroniclers continue during the eighth and ninth centuries to distinguish between the domains of the Bulgars, and those of the Slavs (*Sclaviniae*), though later all this territory came to be known as Bulgaria. Large tracts of land were seized forthwith by the proto-Bulgar aristocracy under Asparukh. Even so, the majority of the Slav peasantry was still free, and serfdom only took root gradually, particularly after the establishment of Christianity under Tsar Boris I. Recent excavations at Devnya (Marcianopolis), in the hinterland of Varna, indicate that in the villages there was a mingling of Slavs and proto-Bulgar settlers at an early stage. Slav and Bulgar inhumations with grave-goods including pottery vessels of both Slav and Bulgar types are found side by side in village sites from the eighth century onwards. Whereas the Slavs normally burnt the corpses of their dead, the Bulgars had a preference for inhumation.

Fig 8

Interesting parallels may be drawn between the domestic architecture of the pagan Slavs in the Balkans, and that of the proto-Bulgars. The huts of the Slavs at this period were rather crude circular or square wattle and daub structures, often sunk into the ground to give the appearance of semi-dugouts. The Bulgars on the other hand favoured the portable leather tent or 'yurt'. These tents were far more decorative and elaborate than is commonly imagined; a stone model of such a 'yurt' on show at the Varna Archaeological Museum is decorated with a graffito representation of a hunting scene, indicating that the walls of yurts were painted or adorned with embroidered panels.

On Asparukh's death in 701, supreme power passed to Khan Tervel,
son or grandson of Asparukh. Tervel continued the Bulgars' expansion-
ist policy in the Balkans, and added parts of eastern Thrace to the new
Slavo-Bulgar state. Tervel was also in a position to intervene in the
internal affairs of Byzantium, through his friendship with an exiled
emperor, Justinian II, who sought refuge at the Bulgar headquarters in
705. This Justinian had had his nose cut off in a Constantinople palace
revolution in 695, hence his nickname of 'Rhinotmetus', and then spent
some years in exile at Cherson on the Black Sea, before marrying the
daughter of the khaqan of the Khazars. Quarrelling with the khaqan,
Justinian fled to Pliska, and persuaded Tervel to support him in a military campaign to regain the throne in Constantinople. Though unable
to breach the capital's mighty walls, Justinian adroitly crept into the city
with a small band of daring followers. Emperor Tiberius II fled panic-
stricken without a struggle, and Justinian regained his palace and the
imperial throne.

Khan Tervel was enthroned by Justinian's side, and granted the title
of 'Caesar'. The Bulgar state won renewal of the tribute payments
inaugurated by Emperor Constantine IV. Thus the Bulgars had
advanced in a quarter of a century, between 680 and 705, from the
Danube estuary right up to the Bosporus and the heart of the imperial
city, and found that they could even make and unmake Byzantine
emperors. As a further recompense for his services, Tervel was allowed
to annex the small but valuable district of Zagoria in northeastern
Thrace, including the hinterland of the Gulf of Burgas.

Tervel proved himself an active and far-sighted ruler. When Emperor
Justinian II turned against his former Bulgar allies in 708 and landed in
Anchialus (Pomorie) with a large Greek force, Tervel launched a
surprise attack which utterly routed the Byzantines. Three years later,
Justinian himself was deposed and assassinated. In 712, Tervel invaded
Thrace and advanced once more to the gates of Constantinople,
retiring home laden with booty.

To the reign of Tervel is also ascribed the capture of the great port of
Varna by the Bulgars. To prevent surprise attacks by the Greek fleet, the
Bulgars built an immense earthwork along the southern portion of
Varna Bay, some 3 kilometres long and 6 metres high. This earthwork
incorporates many fine sculptured stones from the Roman and the

Fig. 7 *Bulgaria at the time of the First Empire (c. AD 900). (After Runciman)*

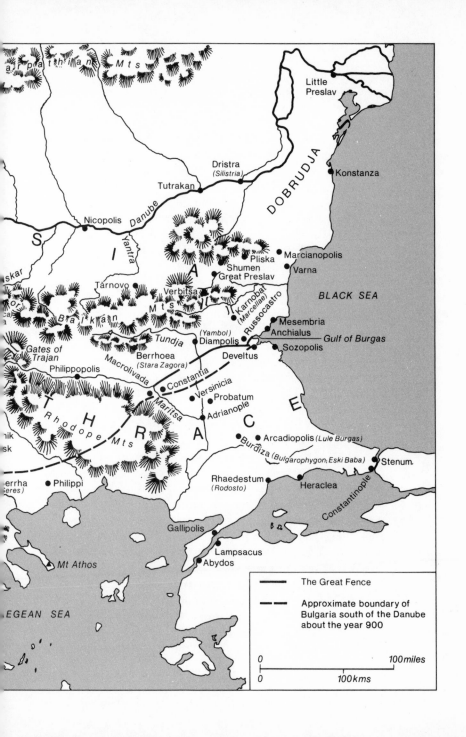

Little
Preslav

Dristra
(Silistria)

Tutrakan

Konstanza

DOBRUDJA

Nicopolis   Danube

S

Yantra

I

Pliska   Marcianopolis

Shumen   Varna

Great Preslav

Tárnovo   Verbitsa   Karnobat
(Marcellae)

A

Mts

Russocastro

BLACK SEA

Ba lkan

Tundja   *(Yambol)*   Mesembria
Diampolis   Anchialus   *Gulf of Burgas*

Gates of   Berrhoea   Develtus   Sozopolis
Trajan   *(Stara Zagora)*

Philippopolis   Macrolivada

Constantia

Versinicia

T   H   Maritsa   Probatum

Rhodope   R   A   Adrianople

Mts   E

Arcadiopolis *(Lule Burgas)*

nik   Burdiza *(Bulgarophygon; Eski Baba)*

sk   Stenum

Philippi   Rhaedestum   Heraclea
(Rodosto)   Constantinople

Gallipolis

Lampsacus

Mt Athos   Abydos

EGEAN SEA

	The Great Fence
- - -	Approximate boundary of Bulgaria south of the Danube about the year 900

0   100 miles

0   100 kms

Byzantine period. It proved valuable in 773, when Emperor Constantine Copronymus attempted a naval attack on Bulgaria with a large fleet, but was foiled.

THE TREATY
WITH
BYZANTIUM

Fig. 7

Under pressure from the Arab caliphate, the feeble Emperor Theodosius III (715–17) sought to neutralize the Bulgar threat by concluding a political and commercial agreement with Khan Tervel, in 716. The terms of this treaty are summarized for us by the Byzantine historian Theophanes. The main political stipulations were that the state frontier should pass along a line later fortified by the Bulgars and known as the Great Fence of Thrace: the line extends from the Gulf of Burgas in the northeast, then through Bakajik, to a point on the river Maritsa about halfway between Philippopolis and Adrianople, reaching at one point the main Belgrade-Constantinople highway. The second article of the treaty provided for annual offerings to the Bulgar khan by the Byzantine court of costly robes and skins, to the value of thirty pounds of gold. The third clause related to return of prisoners by both sides, also mutual extradition of Bulgar or Greek refugees and political suspects, who might seek asylum with the opposing power.

Of exceptional importance was the commercial agreement embodied in article 4 of the Treaty. There was to be free movement and interchange of officially licensed traders between Bulgaria and Byzantium, provided that such merchants were furnished with passports and seals, without which their goods might be confiscated. This convention enabled the Bulgarians to play an increasingly active part in exporting Thracian grain to the Byzantine cities on the Black Sea coast and elsewhere, and in the import of manufactured goods from Constantinople and the Mediterranean world through these ports into the interior of the Balkans.

Emperor Leo the Isaurian, who succeeded the ephemeral Theodosius, ratified the Bulgarian treaty. When the Arabs launched their second great siege of Constantinople, in 717, Khan Tervel aided the Greek defenders by swooping down on the Saracen encampment and slaying up to twenty thousand Arabs, before retiring home laden with booty.

Tervel died in the following year, but is immortalized in one of the three Madara inscriptions which flank the triumphant equestrian figure carved on a high cliff almost within view of the Bulgar capital of Pliska (see Chapter VII). This Greek inscription, carved in the rock-face,

Plates 4, 5

mentions Tervel's services to Emperor Justinian II, his acquisition of the Zagoria region, and his raid on the Saracens besieging Constantinople.

The remainder of the eighth century was a period of comparative stagnation in Bulgarian history, punctuated by wars against Byzantium, and bloody internal strife. Sources are scarce and one or two of the Sublime Khans are known only as shadowy entries in the medieval 'Bulgarian Princes' List', found in Russia. We do not even know the name of Tervel's successor, who reigned from 718 to 725. Then came Khan Sevar, who ruled until 740, and was the last of the great house of Dulo to occupy the throne; with him died out the lineage of Attila the Hun.

A new but short-lived dynasty sprang up with the accession of a bolyar named Kormisosh, of the house of Vokil or Ukil. He is mentioned briefly in the Madara inscriptions. Towards the end of Kormisosh's reign, in 755, the warlike iconoclast emperor of Byzantium, Constantine V, called Copronymus (literally 'Dung-named'), embarked on a forward policy in Thrace. He settled many Armenians and Syrians there, and built fortresses for them to inhabit and defend against the Bulgars. The latter protested; receiving no satisfaction, Kormisosh invaded Byzantine territory right up to the Long Wall of Constantinople. There Constantine Copronymus fell upon the Bulgars with his army and routed them utterly.

Kormisosh died in 756, and was succeeded by his son Vinekh, who had to bear the brunt of disastrous wars with Byzantium. The Bulgars lost patience with his record of defeats, and in 761 they rose up against their khan and massacred him with his family and all the other representatives of the house of Ukil.

In Vinekh's place, the bolyars installed the thirty-year-old Telets, of the house of Ugain. Telets was the leader of the 'war party' in Bulgaria, and ordered a general mobilization, much to the disgust of his Slav subjects, of whom two hundred thousand deserted to seek refuge in Byzantium. In June 763, a great battle was fought near Anchialus (Pomorie); the carnage was immense, but in the end Constantine Copronymus was the victor. Triumphal games were held in the Constantinople circus, and thousands of Bulgar captives slaughtered. A few months later, Telets himself was assassinated, together with the bolyars of his party.

The Bulgarians

After several years of anarchy, the accession of Khan Telerig in 770 stemmed the tide of defeat. Despite a military reverse in 773, Telerig reorganized Bulgaria's military forces, and also turned the tables on Emperor Constantine Copronymus by the exercise of cunning and guile. On one occasion, the Byzantine chronicler Theophanes tells us, Telerig sent a messenger to Constantine to report that opposition activity was rife, and might force him to take refuge in the Byzantine court. Telerig enquired who were the chief secret agents of Byzantium within Bulgaria, to whom he, Telerig, could have recourse in such an emergency. Constantine naïvely sent Telerig a list of Byzantine spies within Bulgaria, whom the khan promptly arrested and put to death. Ironically, Telerig did have to flee the country, in 777; he came to the court of Emperor Leo IV, accepted Christian baptism, and was accorded a Greek bride, a cousin of Empress Irene.

During the reign of Irene and her son Constantine VI in Byzantium, from AD 780 onwards, the Empire had to contend with the capable Khan Kardam (777–802). At first, the Byzantines succeeded in pushing back the Bulgarian frontier to the north. In 784, Empress Irene made an imperial progress from Anchialus, far inland to Berrhoea, the modern Stara Zagora, which she rebuilt and christened Irenupolis. Serdica also remained firmly in Byzantine hands.

In 792, however, Kardam inflicted a disastrous defeat on the youthful Constantine VI at the border fortress of Marcellae. The Byzantine government had once more to submit to paying tribute to the Bulgarians, who periodically raised their demands with blackmailing threats of further military attacks. Constantine VI's failure to check the Bulgarians helped to bring on the crisis of 797, in which Empress Irene had the Emperor, her son, blinded, and assumed autocratic power on her own.

Empress Irene fell from power in 802, and was succeeded by a former *logothete* of the Treasury (or Chancellor of the Exchequer), named Nicephorus. The following year, supreme authority in Bulgaria passed to one of the mightiest of Bulgaria's early rulers, Khan Krum the Conqueror.

Krum is generally considered to have sprung from the lineage of the Bulgar khans of Pannonia, in Central Europe. His youth was occupied in establishing his power in Hungary and Transylvania, where he exploited the valuable salt mines. By about 808, Krum had joined these domains to the old Slavo-Bulgar khanate of Asparukh and his successors, and taken over as supreme master of Pliska. Krum was now sovereign of a realm which stretched from Thrace to the northern Carpathians, and from the lower Sava to the Dniester, and adjoined the Frankish empire of Charlemagne on the Tisza (Theiss). However, a mighty line of Byzantine fortresses, rebuilt by Constantine Copronymus, extended in a semicircle south of the Balkan range, barring the Bulgarian advance into central Thrace and Macedonia; its key points were Serdica, Philippopolis, Adrianople, and Develtus.

In 809, Krum suddenly appeared at the gates of Serdica. In spite of its impressive fortifications and strong garrison, he somehow gained an entry and massacred the defenders, six thousand strong, and numberless civilians. Several Greek officers, including a distinguished military engineer named Eumathius, deserted to the Bulgarian side. This triumph was outweighed, however, by disaster on Krum's home front: Nicephorus had marched straight on Pliska, at the other end of Bulgaria, and found it virtually undefended. The Greeks plundered Krum's palace and retired rejoicing to Constantinople.

This Byzantine triumph was short-lived. In May 811, Emperor Nicephorus set off with his son Stauracius on a great expedition designed to crush the Bulgar menace once for all. On the frontier, at Marcellae, Nicephorus met a delegation of Bulgarian envoys sent by Krum to sue for peace. Dismissing these envoys with contempt, Nicephorus pressed on to Krum's capital of Pliska, which he devastated for a second time. He amused himself by passing Bulgarian babies through threshing machines, and committed other atrocities. In July, Nicephorus rashly pursued the Bulgarian army into a rugged part of the Balkan mountains, and marched into a narrow, steep defile. The Bulgars built wooden palisades at either end of the pass, then fell upon the trapped Byzantines and massacred them wholesale. Emperor Nicephorus perished in the fray. This was a terrible blow to imperial prestige: not since the death of Valens at Adrianople in 378 had an emperor fallen in battle against the barbarians.

Plates 6–8

The head of Nicephorus was exhibited on a stake for some days in front of the jeering Bulgars. Then Krum had it lined with silver and used it as a drinking cup from which to make wassail with his bolyars, to the refrain of the Slavonic toast of '*Zdravitsa*', or 'Good health!'

Stauracius, son and heir to the Byzantine throne, had been mortally wounded in the fray, and it now passed to Michael I Rhangabe. Meanwhile Krum seized Develtus, at the head of the Gulf of Burgas, and deported its inhabitants, including their Christian bishop, into the interior of Bulgaria.

A year later, in 812, Krum sent to Constantinople an ambassador named Dargomer (the first Slav name to feature in the official annals of Bulgaria) to renew the treaty of 716 between Khan Tervel and Emperor Theodosius III. Krum insisted on the extradition of Bulgarian deserters and refugees from Greek territory. On Michael's refusal to hand them over, Krum assaulted the great Black Sea port and emporium of Mesembria (Nessebăr), situated on an almost impregnable peninsula north of Burgas. The Byzantine navy failed to relieve the town, which fell to Krum, along with vast quantities of gold and silver, and stocks of the Byzantine secret weapon known as 'Greek fire', complete with thirty-six syphons from which to project it.

Plates 30–32

In the year following, 813, Emperor Michael I sallied forth to meet Krum in pitched battle, but suffered a crushing defeat at Versinicia. This led to Michael being deposed, and succeeded by the wily Leo the Armenian (813–20). Krum advanced on Constantinople with an immense horde of Slavs and Bulgars, and demanded to be allowed to fix his lance to the Golden Gate, as a token of his supremacy. Leo prepared an ambush for Krum, but the Bulgar khan escaped the assassin's darts, and vowed revenge on the Greeks. As a result, all the suburbs of the city, including the rich towns and villages on the far side of the Golden Horn, and up the European shore of the Bosporus, with their countless churches and monasteries and sumptuous villas, were sent up in flames. The emperor's own palace of St Mamas was looted and burnt, and its ornamented capitals and sculptured animal figures packed up and loaded into wagons to adorn the Bulgar capital of Pliska (see Chapter VII). On his way home, Krum captured Adrianople, and deported most of the surviving inhabitants into Bulgarian domains north of the Danube. Among these captives was an Armenian family with a little boy who by an odd twist of fate was later to become the Byzantine emperor Basil I.

Krum now began to plan the *coup de grâce* against the demoralized Byzantines. Avar auxiliaries poured into Bulgaria from Pannonia, and Slavs assembled from the *Sclaviniae*. Vast siege engines were constructed, also immense catapults, tortoises, battering-rams and ladders. In despair, the Greeks sent envoys to plead for help from the Western Emperor, Louis, in the hope of organizing a 'second front' from the direction of Germany. But on Holy Thursday, 13 April 814, what seemed like a miracle occurred: Krum burst a blood vessel, and the 'new Sennacherib' died a sudden death.

Such was the terror instilled by Krum and his mighty hordes that this aspect has distracted us from his administrative and legislative achieve-ments. Yet we have reason to believe that Krum was a systematic and clever administrator, as is evidenced, for instance, by the Hambarli inscription (now in the Varna Archaeological Museum), which takes the form of a rectangular stone pillar carved with a detailed battle order of the Bulgarian army, inscribed in Greek, but complete with a number of proto-Bulgar official and military titles. The Byzantine encyclopaedia known under the name of Suidas (tenth century) credits Krum with a comprehensive legislative programme, including measures against perjurers and thieves. Preoccupation with social welfare is evident in Krum's injunction that the poor and needy were to be supported by the rich, under pain of confiscation of property. Hearing that the Avar realm had fallen partly as a result of drunkenness among the population, Krum is said to have ordered the rooting up of all vines in Bulgaria – though how this can be reconciled with his taste for drinking wine out of a human skull is hard to explain.

When Omurtag succeeded his father Krum, he was young and in-experienced, and a group of bolyars for a time disputed the succession to the throne of Pliska. By the end of 815, however, Omurtag was firmly established in power. He was to prove one of the most enlightened of Bulgaria's pagan rulers in spite of his cruel persecution of the Christians, dictated largely by political considerations; he was a great builder and patron of the arts.

OMURTAG
THE
BUILDER

Omurtag's first political act was to conclude a thirty years' peace treaty with the Byzantine Empire, whereby he gave up the territory in southern Thrace briefly occupied by Krum, and reverted in the main to the line established earlier by Khan Tervel. The Bulgarians then dug a great ditch and rampart from Develtus (near Burgas on the Black Sea), inland to Macrolivada, and manned it with a string of guard posts.

Omurtag used the respite given by the peace treaty to complete a vast programme of monumental building and public works. He raised for himself a great palace at Pliska, to replace that of his father Krum, burnt down by Emperor Nicephorus. At Transmarisca on the Danube, he built a castle to guard the northern approach to Pliska; to the southwest, he founded in 821 the beautifully situated town and future capital of Great Preslav. In the open countryside not far from Shumen, Omurtag erected the cavalry barracks known as the Aul of Omurtag, consisting of a square walled stockade built of brick, complete with stables for horses, and living quarters inside for picked cavalrymen. A scale model of the Aul may now be seen in the Shumen museum. Halfway between Pliska and the Danube, Omurtag had a mausoleum built for himself.

Peace with Byzantium also enabled the Bulgarians to turn their attention to Western Europe, where they were troubled by the advance of Louis the German, king of the East Franks. In 827 and again in 829, Omurtag invaded Pannonia, and imposed his own governors on the local Slav tribes. Peace in this quarter was not concluded until after Omurtag's death.

Omurtag's reign was a time of ideological and religious crisis and strife. The pagan priests or shamans of the proto-Bulgars, and the heathen priests of Perun, patron deity of the Slavs, joined in suppressing the numerous adepts of Christianity dwelling within Bulgarian territory (many of them former prisoners of war), and also in combatting the influence of the Greek and Frankish Christians from just over the border. Omurtag himself was aware, it would seem, of the prestige which Christianity afforded the Byzantine Emperor and the successors of Charlemagne, as vice-regents of God upon earth. He adopted the title of 'Arkhon, or sovereign, by the grace of God', even though the supreme pagan god, not the God of the Christians, was meant. Yet reasons of state demanded massive persecutions of the Christians. Among those who died a martyr's death were four bishops, including Archbishop Manuel of Adrianople, and 377 other captives. Their memory was celebrated annually in Constantinople on January 22, and their martyrdom described in the Greek *Synaxarium*.

Plates 6–8

Fig. 23

The most determined enemies of Christianity, apart from the priests themselves, were the Bulgar bolyars or noblemen. The Slavonic population was more responsive to Christian propaganda, much of it emanating from descendants of the original Byzantine Christians, whose forbears had survived the waves of invasion in the Balkans. A certain amount of intermingling of the Slavonic peasant and chieftain classes with these old local elements was certainly taking place by this period.

Of particular interest is a short choral Office in honour of the Bulgarian martyrs, discovered in the Vatican Library, and published by Enrica Follieri in 1963. The hymnographer, evidently a contemporary of these tragic events, was called Joseph, and is probably to be identified with Joseph of Studios, a noted Byzantine author. The hymn indicates clearly the varied ethnic and social background of the Bulgarian martyrs of this period.

In spite of his occasional cruelties, Omurtag remains one of the most fascinating of all Bulgar rulers. None but a philosopher, albeit a pagan one, could have dictated the words found on a granite column now embodied in the Church of the Forty Martyrs at Great Tărnovo:

Man dies, even though he lives nobly, and another is born; and let the latest born, seeing this, remember him who made it. The name of the prince is Omurtag, the Sublime Khan. God grant that he live a hundred years.

However, Omurtag was not fated to live for a century: he died compara‚ tively young in 831, after reigning for sixteen years.

Under Omurtag's successors Malamir (831–36) and Pressian (836–52) the Bulgarians penetrated further into Macedonia, and annexed large areas of what is now southern Yugoslavia. The internal crisis resulting from the spread of Christianity, and the exacerbated reaction of the pagan priests, continued at boiling point, and even led to the execution of Prince Enravotas, a brother of Khan Malamir, who was converted to Christianity by a Greek captive from Adrianople.

A new era in Bulgarian history was inaugurated in 852, with the accession of Khan Boris, who later assumed the name of Michael on his conversion to the Christian faith. The early part of Boris's reign was

EARLY CHRISTIAN‚ ITY: KNYAZ BORIS‚ MICHAEL

Fig. 8

Fig. 8 Prince Boris-Michael. Miniature from a manuscript of the Didactic Gospel of Constantine of Preslav, in the Moscow Historical Museum. (After Naslednikova)

occupied with unsuccessful campaigns against the Frankish empire and its Eastern satellites, notably the Croats. Later Boris attempted, unsuccessfully, to annex areas of Serbia and what is now Albania.

As the years went by, Boris became aware of the spiritual bankruptcy of traditional Bulgarian paganism, which had become more and more associated with social backwardness, illiteracy and also with potential feudal resistance to the royal power. Paganism, by the mid-ninth century, appeared clearly inferior both spiritually and politically to Orthodox and Catholic Christianity alike, as well as to the splendid edifice of Islam under the Arab caliphs, the triumphant Commanders of the Faithful. Not only did Christianity offer cultural and social progress through the introduction of literacy and a disciplined way of life, but it provided a framework for the aggrandisement of the monarchy: in Byzantine Christianity, especially, the sovereign was conceived of as a divinely anointed autocrat and a lay pontiff with supreme authority not only over State and People, but over the Holy Church itself. For a country to remain pagan, on the other hand, was to opt for political weakness and social barbarism.

Leaving aside reasons of state, there is no need to question Boris's religious conviction, when the moment came to make his decision. Boris had witnessed and heard of the heroism of the Christian martyrs put to death during preceding reigns - heroism which won international renown, and brought disgrace and shame upon the cruel, heathen Bulgarians in the eyes of the world. Boris had certainly heard much of the sublimity of the Orthodox liturgy, as celebrated in Saint Sophia cathedral in Constantinople and other shrines well known to Bulgarian merchants and travellers. There is a story told in the *Russian Primary Chronicle* concerning the conversion of the Russians in the tenth century. Prince Vladimir sends envoys to various peoples in search of the true faith. The Russian envoys report unfavourably on the Volga Bulgars and the Germans, but add:

> Then we went to the Greeks [to Constantinople], and they led us to the place where they worship their God; and we knew not whether we were in heaven, or on earth. For on earth there is no such vision nor beauty, and we do not know how to describe it; we know only that there God dwells among men.

How different were these splendours of St Sophia from the crude mouthings of Bulgaria's pagan *shamans*!

While Boris was pondering these matters, a violent religious and political conflict had set the Papacy and the Constantinople patriarchate at loggerheads. It was the ambition of Pope Nicholas I (858–67) to reassert the supremacy of Rome over the entire Church Universal. His refusal to recognize the legitimate succession of the Constantinople patriarch Photius culminated in 863 in formal excommunication of the latter, in response to which Photius made the audacious gesture of excommunicating Nicholas.

Just at this time, Prince Rastislav of Moravia sent envoys to Emperor Michael III in Constantinople, in search of a military and political alliance. To head the return mission to Moravia, the emperor's choice fell on two eminent brothers from Thessalonica, Constantine (Cyril) and Methodius, to whom the Slavonic peoples are indebted for their conversion to Christianity, and for the invention of the earliest Slavonic alphabets, the Cyrillic and the Glagolitic.

Boris of Bulgaria was still toying with the idea of officially embracing Christianity. One account ascribes his final conversion to a Greek slave called Theodore Cupharas, who taught Boris to pray to the God of the Christians and thus avert a terrible famine which threatened Bulgaria with starvation. Another version of the events gives the credit to a Christian painter named Methodius (not to be confused with the missionary from Thessalonica), who terrified Boris by a realistic mural painting of the Last Judgement.

It fell to Boris to make a choice between Rome and Byzantium, the two founts of Christian dogma and discipline. Early in the 860s, Boris evidently undertook to receive Christianity at the hands of the Frankish Catholic clergy. This decision had clear-cut political implications. The danger of Carolingian influence spreading right into Thrace, within easy reach of Constantinople, seriously alarmed the Byzantines. Emperor Michael III determined on a military demonstration, moving an army to the Bulgarian frontier, and sending a fleet along Bulgaria's Black Sea littoral. The Greeks demanded the abandonment of the Frankish alliance, and the conversion of the khan of Bulgaria to the Orthodox persuasion.

The Bulgarian military position was precarious, and the country suffering from famine, so Boris capitulated at once. In 864 (or, according to some authorities, in 865), the Bulgarian khan received baptism at the hands of priests sent from Constantinople, taking the name of Michael after that of the Byzantine emperor who stood as his sponsor and godfather. Boris abandoned the pagan Turkic title of khan for the Slavonic 'knyaz' or chief prince. Mass conversion of the people, often by force, followed. A pagan insurrection headed by many leading Bulgar bolyars was crushed with severity, no less than fifty-two ringleaders being executed together with their families.

This first honeymoon between the Byzantine and Bulgarian Churches ended in bitterness and rupture. Antagonized by Greek arrogance, Boris-Michael decided to renew his former links with the West. In the summer of 866, he sent envoys both to the court of Louis the German at Ratisbon, and to Pope Nicholas I in Rome. To the Pope he forwarded a set of 106 questions on theological, social, also legal and political matters, together with a plea for an independent patriarch for the Bulgarian Church.

Boris-Michael's questionnaire to the Pope reflects the usual mixture of bewilderment and occasional resentment, combined with an honest desire to please, which marks the response of simple pagans the world over, when exposed to the threats and blandishments of well-meaning Christian missionaries. For all their occasional naivety, Boris-Michael's questions to Pope Nicholas, taken together with the Pontiff's answers, provide one of the most interesting documents we possess on social conditions in the First Bulgarian Empire. Were the Byzantines correct, asked Boris-Michael, in imposing fasts on Wednesdays as well as on Fridays, and in banning baths on both days? (This love of bathing among the Bulgars is also demonstrated by the elaborate hypocausts which existed at the residence of Khans Krum and Omurtag at Pliska.) Should they wear their belts while taking communion, and remove their turbans in church? Must they abandon their fashion of wearing trousers? How were they to dispose of their surplus wives, in view of the widespread custom of polygamy among the pagan Bulgars? Was sexual intercourse permitted on Sundays or not? Were laymen allowed to conduct public prayers for rain, or only priests, and could ordinary people make the sign of the Cross over the table before a meal? How many true patriarchs were there, and was it true that Constantinople ranked in the hierarchy immediately after Rome?

Plate 8

The Pope's exhaustive replies to these and many other questions are most interesting. Nicholas chided Boris-Michael for the severity of his punishment of civil offenders, and urged him to abandon the use of torture in criminal proceedings. Forced conversion to Christianity should be replaced by persuasion. The Pope condemned various pagan practices described in Boris-Michael's questionnaire, such as the use of a horse's tail as a banner for the army, the seeking of auguries, the casting of spells, and the performance of ceremonial songs and dances before battle, as well as the taking of oaths on a sword. The Bulgarians were also urged to give up their superstitious practice of seeking cures from a miraculous stone, and wearing amulets round their necks as a protection against sickness. As for the status of the patriarchal see of Constantinople, Nicholas dismissed its apostolic pretensions contemptuously, and was scathing in regard to its claim for monopoly of production of the Holy Chrism. On the setting-up of an independent Bulgarian Church, Nicholas was prudently evasive, indicating that everything depended on the Christian prowess of the newly converted Bulgarian nation.

A rapid sequence of events now led up to a definitive swing by the fickle Bulgarians back towards the fold of Byzantine Orthodoxy. Pope

Nicholas firmly refused to ratify Boris-Michael's choice of a Roman Catholic primate for the infant Bulgarian Church, insisting that the appointment of bishops for Bulgaria was an exclusive papal prerogative. By the summer of 867, prior to the death of Pope Nicholas and the accession of Hadrian II, Bulgarian relations with Rome became strained.

Meanwhile, in Constantinople, a palace revolution took place in September 867, in the course of which Emperor Michael III was murdered by his favourite protégé, the future Basil I, himself an Armenian who had spent part of his childhood as a captive in Bulgaria. Basil deposed Patriarch Photius and reinstated his rival Ignatius. Since Ignatius was *persona grata* with the Papacy, his appointment restored communion between Constantinople and Rome. A council of the Oecumenical Church, attended by representatives of Pope Hadrian II, was held in Constantinople during 869 and 870, and decided that Bulgaria should depend on the Greek patriarchate of Constantinople, and thus Bulgaria duly receive her semi-autonomous archbishop and subordinate clerics from the metropolitan see of Byzantine Christendom.

The next landmark in the history of Bulgarian Christianity occurred in 885, when Methodius died in Moravia, his whole work apparently on the brink of failure. Methodius had towards the end of his life fallen out with the Papacy, partly as a result of his refusal to tolerate any tampering with the Nicene Creed. The death of Methodius meant the end of the Slavonic liturgy in Central Europe. He had named his ablest disciple Gorazd as his successor, but Gorazd was unable to maintain his position in face of relentless opposition from the Latin and German clergy, egged on by the Moravian Prince Svatopluk I. The leaders of the Slavonic Church in Moravia – Gorazd, Clement, Nahum, Angelarius, Laurentius and Sabbas – were imprisoned; some of them were then deported, and on reaching Belgrade, were warmly welcomed by Boris-Michael's viceroy there, who sent them on to Pliska. Other survivors of the Slavonic Moravian Church reached the Bulgarian capital via Venice, where they had been sold as slaves, and redeemed by Byzantine envoys acting on behalf of Emperor Basil I.

About 886, Clement was sent from Pliska to Macedonia, with instructions to baptize any who were still pagans, to celebrate the liturgy in the Slavonic tongue, translate Greek religious texts, and train a native clergy. The centre of his activity was the district of Devol (in present/ day Albania), between Lake Ohrida and the Adriatic; after consecra/ tion as bishop in 893, Clement concentrated on the Ohrida area itself. Thanks to Clement's exemplary labours over a period of thirty years, Macedonia (above all Ohrida) became a leading centre of Slavonic Christian culture, and a hearth of early Bulgarian civilization.

At first, Clement's comrade Nahum remained in northeastern Bulgaria, where, both in Pliska and at the royal monastery of St Pante/ leimon (Patleina) close to Preslav, he helped to found another school of Old Bulgarian literature, until transferred to Macedonia in 893 to assist Clement in his educational and missionary labours. The importance of Clement, Nahum and their associates in laying the foundations of Old Bulgarian literature and Christian culture is examined in more detail in Chapter VI.

In 889 after a reign of thirty/seven years – one of the longest in Bulgaria's annals – Boris abdicated and retired to a monastery, possibly that of St Panteleimon at Preslav. The throne passed to Vladimir, eldest son of Boris, who immediately abandoned most of his father's policies in favour of a return to paganism, in which he was encouraged by the reactionary Bulgar bolyars. Court life became extravagant and de/ bauched, and the Byzantine alliance was abandoned for a pact with the German emperor Arnulf.

The reign of this Bulgarian equivalent of Julian the Apostate lasted four years, until 893, when Boris was finally provoked to the point of rallying the faithful against his own son. After having Vladimir blinded and imprisoned, Boris summoned a general assembly of the nation, which proclaimed Boris's younger son, the monk Symeon, as ruler, annulling Symeon's monastic vows. From now on, Slavonic replaced Greek as official language of the Bulgarian State, and the capital of the country was moved from Pliska, with its pagan associations, to Preslav, which Boris had already beautified with churches and monasteries, workshops and *scriptoria*.

SYMEON THE STRONG

Plates 18–21, *Figs. 30–33*

Under the reign of Tsar Symeon, which lasted more than thirty years, the might of the First Bulgarian Empire reached a new peak, equalling the epic age of Khan Krum. Symeon had originally been trained for the post of archbishop of Bulgaria. Raised in Constantinople, as a royal hostage, he followed courses at the University installed in the Magnaura palace. He became a proficient Greek scholar, with a taste for the works of Aristotle and Demosthenes; later he came to favour the Fathers of the Christian Church.

On emerging from his cell to take over the Bulgarian throne from his blinded brother, Vladimir, Symeon soon adapted himself to the outside world, and the requirements of statecraft and war. Towards the end of his life, indeed, he developed a streak of militaristic megalomania. Like Krum before him, Symeon dreamed of founding a new Slavo-Byzantine empire centred on Constantinople, the head of which would be himself, a Bulgarian, arrayed in the imperial purple of the Greeks.

Meanwhile, Symeon set out to transform Preslav into a second Constantinople. According to a contemporary writer, John the Exarch, visitors to Preslav were overcome by the sight of all the great

Plates 18–21, Figs. 30–33

churches and palaces, decorated with marbles and frescoes, and depicting the sights of heaven, the stars, sun and moon as well as flowers and trees and the fishes of the deep. In the midst of all this splendour sat Symeon himself, enthroned 'in a garment studded with pearls, a chain of medals round his neck and bracelets on his wrists, girt with a purple belt, and having a golden sword by his side'. John the Exarch adds that any rustic Bulgarian tourist who glimpsed these sights would return home, disenchanted with the simplicity of his own humble cottage, but eager to tell his friends about the wonders of Symeon's new city.

War with Byzantium broke out in 894, the year after Symeon's accession. The immediate *casus belli* was a commercial dispute. Since Khan Tervel's commercial treaty of 716, there had existed a regular Bulgarian trade depot in Constantinople, protected by special imperial privileges. Under Tsars Boris and Symeon, the Bulgarians came to depend increasingly on export outlets for their local products – wines, beasts, corn, timber and many other commodities – and the chief outlet was Constantinople. In exchange, the Bulgarians imported Byzantine and oriental manufactured products, such as dyed silk, jewellery and porcelain, also spices. A crisis arose when the courtier Stylianus Zautses, Logothete of the Drome, encouraged two Greek merchants to establish a monopoly of Greek trade with Bulgaria, the depot for which they transferred from Constantinople to Thessalonica, where heavy taxes were imposed on Bulgarian goods.

Symeon demanded compensation for losses sustained. Rebuffed, Symeon invaded Thrace and marched on Constantinople. Emperor Leo VI responded by sending envoys to the Magyars, who at this time were encamped north of the Danube estuary, in the plain of Bessarabia. The Magyars were ferried across the Danube by the Greek fleet, and advanced on Preslav, forcing Symeon to abandon his march on Constantinople and hurry northwards to defend his own capital. Symeon in his turn persuaded the dreaded Turkic Pechenegs to attack the Magyars from the direction of the Dnieper, forcing them to move westwards over the Carpathians into the Pannonian plain, where they founded the medieval kingdom of Hungary.

Peace was concluded in 897 on terms quite favourable to Bulgaria, including provision for an annual tribute of gifts to be rendered to Symeon by the Greeks. This treaty lasted for fifteen years, until Leo VI's death in 912. Then Leo's brother, the short-lived alcoholic emperor Alexander, insulted Symeon's envoys sent to renew the 897 treaty. War broke out, and lasted with intervals until Symeon's death in 927. On one occasion, in 924, Symeon reached the walls of Constantinople and engaged in personal parley with Emperor Romanus Lecapenus.

An interesting source for the history of the period is the exchange of letters between Patriarch Nicholas of Constantinople and his erstwhile brother in Christ, the renegade monk Symeon, now prince of the hosts of Bulgaria. These letters, alternately threatening and cajoling, and Symeon's disrespectful, bantering replies, illustrate the paradoxical character of this Christian ruler whom fate had turned into the bitterest foe of Byzantium – the fount of Bulgaria's new Christian culture. At times, Symeon acted as a worthy candidate for the imperial crown of Byzantium; at others, he behaved like the veritable descendant of Attila the Hun, reverting to the uncouth ways of his ancestors.

Symeon was the creator of both the Bulgarian Empire, and the Bulgarian patriarchate. In 925, he proclaimed himself Emperor and Autocrat of the Romans and the Bulgars, a title ratified by the Pope, and revived later under the Second Bulgarian Empire. (By the Romans, are meant the Byzantine Greeks and their subject races.) In 926, Symeon proclaimed the independence of the Bulgarian Church within the Orthodox communion, under its own patriarch, the former Archbishop Leontius.

Out of the ordinary in so many respects, Symeon was remarkable even in the manner of his death. In May 927, a Greek astrologer told Emperor Romanus Lecapenus that the thread of Symeon's life was bound up with the existence of a certain marble column in the Constantinople forum. On May 27, Romanus, as an experiment, had this column's capital removed. At this same hour, Tsar Symeon died of heart failure. Apocryphal though it may be, this story gives some impression of the awe inspired by this larger than lifesize, controversial ruler.

It was under Symeon that the military and government machinery of the First Bulgarian Empire reached its greatest size and complexity. Although no comprehensive survey of this machinery exists, yet we can piece together from various sources and inscriptions a fair picture of the salient features of this state structure.

Slavonic and proto-Bulgar titles continued to exist side by side for over a century after Bulgaria's conversion, while ecclesiastical ranks are largely taken from the Greek. To give a few examples, we find that under Boris-Michael the Sublime Khan becomes *Knyaz* or Prince, a Slavonic title used in Russia up to modern times; Symeon assumed the title of Tsar or Emperor. The Bulgar aristocracy of the *boïlyas* or *bolyars* had their name transformed into the Slavonic form *boyar*. Tribal chiefs bore the Slavonic title *zhupan*, a princely dignity even better known in medieval Serbia. Constantine Porphyrogenitus refers to a high military officer termed 'Alo-Bogotur', embodying the Turkic *bagatur* (Russian, *bogatyr*), meaning a hero. From the end of the ninth century dates a handsome lead seal of a certain Bulgar Khan-Bagatur Irtkhituin; the seal, which is illustrated in Vasil Gyuzelev's biography of Boris I, is adorned with a Christian cross. Around AD 950, we encounter the *Fig. 9* tombstone of a certain Mostich, with an important Slavonic inscription mentioning that he was *chărgoboïlya* (officer in charge of state security) under Tsars Symeon and Peter, and had retired at the age of eighty to become a monk.

Sometimes high Bulgarian officials would be known to the Byzantines by Greek equivalents of their Bulgarian titles; thus the Bulgarian *tarkhan* of Belgrade is referred to in the Life of St Clement of Ohrida as *hypostrategus* or military governor-general of the province. Greek ranks and titles, for obvious reasons, predominated in the Bulgarian Church.

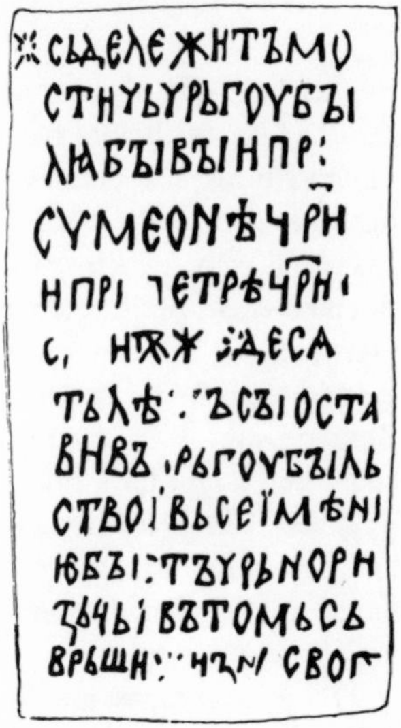

Fig. 9 Tombstone of Mostich, a retired state official, who died about AD 950. It bears an important early Cyrillic inscription. (After Stanchev)

Apart from such common terms as those of patriarch or bishop ('episkop'), we find in Bulgaria the title of *exarch*, also that of *syncellus*. The latter was, in Byzantium, a high cleric, who often acceded later to the patriarchate; he was appointed by the emperor in agreement with the patriarch, and was instituted with much pomp at a ceremony in the imperial palace. The syncellus, in Byzantium at least, took precedence over all the ordinary officials and acted as a kind of liaison officer between the emperor and the patriarch.

It has to be noted, however, that in spite of the elaborate structure of State power under Symeon, the commercial and financial base remained primitive and weak. Although the later rulers of the First Bulgarian Empire made lead, silver and gold seals for ceremonial and business use, none of them attempted to strike coins in their own name. They remained slavishly dependent on the Byzantine currency and on barter. An independent coinage did not evolve in Bulgaria until after the establishment of the Second Bulgarian Empire at Tărnovo, at the very end of the twelfth century.

Symeon's imperial title and grandiose conquests had been bought at too high a price. The country was exhausted. Symeon's successor, Tsar Peter, was physically a weakling, under whom Bulgaria rapidly fell

DECLINE
UNDER TSAR
PETER

into decline. The Byzantines wisely bided their time; they even established a form of alliance with Bulgaria by granting young Tsar Peter an imperial bride, the Princess Maria, granddaughter of Romanus Lecapenus, known in the annals of Bulgaria as Empress Irene.

Peter's reign, which lasted from 927 to 969, was one of the longest but most disastrous in Bulgarian history. The country lay inert, a passive prey to savage invaders from the north. In 934, for instance, the Magyars made a deep incursion into the Balkans, and reached Develtus, near Burgas; so great was the number of their captives that a pretty woman could be bought for a silk dress. The humbler classes were restless; in 930, Peter's brother Michael escaped from the monastic cell to which he had been relegated, and made off to the western mountains, where he founded a kind of brigand kingdom aided by large bands of Slav malcontents.

This general unrest also found expression in a most wide-spread and politically dangerous heresy, that of Bogomilism. This will be dealt with in more detail in Chapter V, and here it will suffice to observe that the Bogomils taught that matter was the creation of the devil, and that the service of principalities and powers was anathema to God, as was the whole structure and hierarchy of the Orthodox Church. As so often before and since (and we have only to think of the French Huguenots or Cromwell's Puritan Roundheads), religious dissent gave rise to militant social action; and in the absence of anything like modern political parties, the pent-up resentment of the underprivileged found an outlet in Bogomilism as a new, exciting form of religious protest.

Towards the end of his life, in 965, Peter made a diplomatic blunder which was to plunge Bulgaria into fresh misery. He sent envoys to Constantinople to demand from the new, warlike Emperor Nicephorus Phocas (963–69) a resumption of the subsidy which the Byzantines had formerly paid to the Bulgarian Sublime Khans, and which the Greeks had renewed in the form of a dowry when Tsar Peter of Bulgaria married the Greek princess Maria-Irene in 927. But Maria-Irene had just died, and Nicephorus Phocas professed himself highly insulted at this Bulgarian demand for what was described as 'the customary tribute'. Nicephorus and his courtier poured abuse on the Bulgarian ambassadors, terming them 'filthy beggars', and cursing their master, Tsar Peter, as being no emperor, but a princeling clad in skins.

Possibly this was but a form of diplomatic provocation, designed to prepare the way for unleashing upon the enfeebled Bulgarians the military might of the Russians and Varangians, who constituted a regular threat to Constantinople through their superior naval strength. Peter did his best to fend off the approaching menace, sending his two sons Boris and Romanus as hostages to Constantinople. But Nicephorus continued with his plans; he sent an envoy to the Russian court in Kiev, bearing a subsidy of 1,500 pounds of gold, as an inducement to the heathen Prince Svyatoslav to cross the Danube and invade Bulgaria from the north.

In August 967, Prince Svyatoslav crossed the Danube with the imperial ambassador Calocyras as guide, and sixteen thousand men. Svyatoslav overran the north of Bulgaria, capturing twenty-four towns, and then set up a war-time capital at Khan Asparukh's old fortress of Little Preslav on the Danube. Svyatoslav took such a fancy to this region that he seriously thought of moving his capital permanently from Kiev to Little Preslav, which he found a most attractive spot; it was also an important economic centre, receiving silver, fabrics, wines and fruits from Greece; silver and horses from Bohemia and Hungary; and skins, wax, honey and slaves from Russia itself.

THE RUSSIANS IN BULGARIA

Marching south, Svyatoslav captured Great Preslav in 969, proceeding thence to storm Philippopolis (Plovdiv), the metropolis of Thrace. Emperor Nicephorus realized that the situation had got thoroughly out of hand, and that the Russians would soon be appearing at the gates of Constantinople by land, as they had already several times appeared by ship. Another disquieting factor was the news that Patrician Calocyras, the imperial ambassador, had turned traitor, and was seeking to make a bid for the imperial throne of Constantinople.

Nicephorus was indeed in dire peril, but the blow when it fell on the night of 10 December 969 came from within his own household. Empress Theophano had taken as her lover the Armenian general John Tzimiskes, who was the moving spirit in a palace plot that put an end to Nicephorus's life as well as to his warlike plans, which were to be worthily continued by Tzimiskes himself. It is interesting to note that Tzimiskes, who was to extinguish the First Empire in Eastern Bulgaria, was born in a small Armenian town called Khozan in Anatolia, which later adopted the emperor's name – Tshmishkatzak. He was a great-nephew of an outstanding Armenian general in the Byzantine service, the Grand Domestic John Curcuas.

John Tzimiskes immediately turned his attention to the situation in the Balkans, deputing the half-Armenian Bardas Sclerus to take charge of operations. In Bulgaria, Tsar Peter had died in 969, to be succeeded by his son Boris II, who had been sent back from Constantinople.

The Russian prince Svyatoslav failed to take the measure of Tzimiskes's military genius, and sent insolent messages to Constantinople, affecting to order the Byzantines out of Europe altogether, unless an enormous tribute was paid. In the spring of 971, at the head of a large and well-trained army, Tzimiskes set out on one of the most brilliant campaigns in Byzantine history. In April he took Great Preslav from the Russians after a furious battle. Svyatoslav's men then fell back to the Danube and fortified themselves in Silistra (Dristra, Dorystolum). After three months of siege the Russians and Varangians were worn out by the assaults of the Byzantine crack troops and harassment by fire-shooting ships of the imperial Byzantine navy on the Danube. Svyatoslav capitulated, and negotiated an armistice to allow himself and his followers to return unmolested to his capital of Kiev, pledging himself never again to attack Byzantium, Bulgaria, or the Byzantine Black Sea port of Cherson. But he was ambushed by the Pechenegs on his homeward journey and slain in battle close to the Dnieper rapids, in 972.

Tzimiskes returned to Constantinople, taking with him the Bulgarian royal family and great quantities of booty, to celebrate a traditional victor's triumph in the city. Instead of riding in the imperial chariot drawn by four white horses, he set in his own place of honour a greatly venerated icon of the Virgin, which he had brought with him from Bulgaria; the Emperor himself followed devoutly behind. During the ceremony, Tzimiskes stripped the Bulgarian Tsar Boris of the insignia of royalty, but raised him to the rank of *magister* in the Byzantine hierarchy. Boris's brother Romanus was castrated, to disqualify him from attempting to restore the Bulgarian monarchy. The Bulgarian Church now also lost its independent status, at least in eastern Bulgaria. The separate Bulgarian patriarchate was suppressed for the time being after an existence of less than half a century; the Bulgarian Church was re-organized under Greek bishops sent from Constantinople.

Emperor Tzimiskes distinguished himself further by conquests in TSAR SAMUEL Anatolia and the Levant, but perished – probably poisoned – in 976 AND THE while still in his prime. The death of this formidable warrior provoked a TWILIGHT OF sudden revival of Bulgarian independence, centred on the western EMPIRE regions of Macedonia. It is a remarkable coincidence that this resurgence of Bulgarian independence was headed by a family of four brothers of wholly or partly Armenian descent – as in the case of Emperor Tzimiskes, who had overthrown the Bulgarian realm of Symeon, Peter and Boris II. These four brothers, David, Moses, Aaron and Samuel, are commonly known as the Comitopuli, their father Nicholas being a provincial *comes* or count, possibly governor of Sofia. Their mother's name was Hripsimé, a common and exclusively Armenian name, taken from that of one of the holiest martyrs of the early Armenian Church.

Samuel and his brothers raised the standard of revolt in the name of the legitimate Bulgarian king, Boris II, who somehow made his way from Byzantium to Bulgaria, but was accidentally shot dead by a Bulgarian sentry. Two of Samuel's brothers perished, while Aaron was murdered by his brother Samuel, who suspected him of treason. Thus by the end of the century Samuel was unrivalled master of a new Bulgarian empire, based largely on Macedonia.

Samuel's empire had its centre first at Prespa, later on at Ohrida, where he re-established the Bulgarian patriarchate, after its various peregrinations to Sofia, Vodena, Moglena and Prespa; as an ecclesiastical centre, Ohrida was to survive Samuel's empire by several centuries, and is now one of the glories of southern Yugoslavia.

It was not until 993, after several victories over the Byzantines in Thessaly and near Sofia, that Samuel finally assumed the title of Tsar. Samuel conquered the Serbian territories as far as Zara on the Adriatic, and also took the Srem region from the Magyars. Other acquisitions included the northern half of Greece with Epirus, much of Albania, including Dyrrachium (the modern Durazzo) and finally Rascia and Dioclea. In 997, Samuel briefly reoccupied Bulgaria's original heartland, the region of Pliska and Preslav, and the hinterland of Varna, only to lose it again to the Byzantine emperor, Basil II, in 1001. Geographically, Samuel's strength lay in the Macedonian kernel of his realm, oriented towards the west and the south, though in most respects Samuel's short-lived empire was a true successor to that of Tsar Symeon.

After 1001, the fortunes of war began to turn against Samuel. Follow, ing his successful campaigns against the rebellious aristocracy of Asia Minor, and the Muslim Fatimids in Syria, Basil II undertook a number of campaigns, each of which resulted in the detaching of a province from the Bulgarian empire. Despite the stubborn resistance of the population, in which the Bogomil heretics also played their part, the Greeks systematically reconquered all Bulgaria's northeastern territories, as well as Thessaly and the regions of Sofia (Sredets) and the Danube stronghold of Vidin. Some of the boyars wavered in their allegiance to Samuel, and began to pass over to the Byzantine emperor.

The fighting continued indecisively for several years. Emperor Basil II took advantage of a lull to reinforce his army, and to bribe more of the Bulgarian magnates to desert Samuel's cause. In the 1014 campaign in the Belassitsa Mountains, the Bulgarian army was attacked in the rear, taken by surprise and utterly defeated. Fourteen thousand warriors were taken prisoner, and Samuel himself barely escaped with his life. Basil II blinded all the prisoners, except for one man in every hundred, who was to have one eye left, so that he could lead his comrades back home to their sovereign. The terrible sight of these men caused Tsar Samuel to die of shock. Basil's ruthlessness earned him the title of 'Bulgaroktonos' or 'the Bulgar,slayer', of which he was very proud.

Samuel's son Gabriel Radomir reigned for only one year, from 1014 to 1015, before being murdered by his cousin Ivan Vladislav, who occu, pied the throne from 1015 to 1018. Ivan Vladislav who left an important Slavonic inscription at Bitolya to posterity perished in battle at Dyrra, chium, thus bringing independent Bulgaria's death struggle to an end. Basil II made a ceremonial entry into Ohrida, receiving homage from the Tsar's widow and the other surviving members of the royal house. The whole Balkan peninsula now belonged to the Byzantine Empire, for the first time since the Slavonic migrations almost five centuries before.

Fig. 10

Fig. 10 Part of Slavonic inscription of Tsar Ivan Vladislav on stone block, from Bitolya (AD 1015–1016). (After Zaimov)

CHAPTER IV

The Rise and Fall of the Second Bulgarian Empire

The subjection of Bulgaria to direct Byzantine rule lasted rather more than a century and a half, until 1185, though it was punctuated by a series of rebellions.

It must be conceded that the civil policy of Emperor Basil II the Bulgar-Slayer towards the defeated Bulgarians was as moderate as his behaviour towards his defeated foe on the battlefield had been cruel and brutal. In view of the wide-spread devastation throughout the Balkans, Basil exempted the Bulgarians from paying taxes in gold and silver, and accepted instead payment in kind, in the form of beasts, agricultural products and other local commodities.

Byzantium's newly conquered Bulgarian territory was now divided into administrative districts, which were called 'themes'. The capital was established at Skoplje, the governor-general of which had the exalted title of 'strategus'. Among other important provinces was that of Paristrion or Paradunavon on the Danube, with its capital at Silistra. The region on the Adriatic coast, which had belonged to Bulgaria under Tsar Samuel, now formed the theme of Dalmatia. Some years later, around 1067, we find mention of the Byzantine theme or province of Serdica, whose *dux* was then the future emperor Romanus Diogenes.

The Bulgarian patriarchate of Ohrida was down-graded to an archbishopric. However, the special privileges of this Church founda-tion were retained under the new dispensation. The Ohrida arch-bishopric was recognized as autocephalous within the Byzantine hier-archy, and its incumbent was appointed personally by the Byzantine emperor, not by the Oecumenical patriarch of Constantinople.

Vivid, not to say scandalous sidelights on the relations between the Byzantine clerics and their Bulgarian and Macedonian flock are given in the letters of the Greek Archbishop Theophylact of Ohrida, who flourished at the end of the eleventh century and composed a biography of his predecessor, St Clement of Ohrida. In one epistle, Archbishop Theophylact remarks to his correspondent:

By saying that you have thoroughly become a barbarian among the Bulgarians, you, dearest friend, say aloud what I myself dream in my sleep. Because – think of it – how much I have drunk from the cup of vulgarity, being so far away from the lands of wisdom, and how much I have imbibed owing to the prevailing lack of culture! Since we have been living for a long time in the land of the Bulgarians, vulgarity has become our close companion and mate.

The Bulgarians, we gather, had driven Theophylact to drink. In another of these outspoken epistles, he scornfully refers to the Bulgarians as 'unclean barbarians, smelling of hides, poorer in their way of life than they are rich in evil disposition'. Writing to his subordinate, the Bishop of Vidin, Theophylact exclaims:

> And so do not lose heart, as if you were the only one to suffer! Are there Cuman tribes invading your land? What are they, however, in comparison with the local people of Ohrida who come out from the city to attack us! Have you got treacherous citizens? Yours are nothing but children in comparison with our own citizens, Bulgarians that they are!

Genuine sympathy between the Greek master race and the Bulgarian population was assuredly lacking. Latent antipathies flared up after Basil II's death, largely as a result of the rapacious fiscal policy of Emperor Michael IV the Paphlagonian (1034–41). Taxes were steadily increased, and had now to be paid in hard cash. The local Greek governors enriched themselves as quickly as possible and then retired home to enjoy their spoils; peasants were snatched from the fields, and conscripted to fight in remote lands against the foes of the Byzantine Empire.

DELYAN'S REBELLION

The financial policy of the central government provoked the Slavs of the Balkans to break out in revolt. When the Slav Archbishop of Ohrida, John, died in 1037, a Greek named Leo was appointed in his place. The rebellion which now broke out soon took on dangerous proportions. A pretender named Peter Delyan, grandson of Tsar Samuel and probably a son of the Bulgarian ruler Gabriel Radomir, was proclaimed tsar in Belgrade in 1040. When Prince Alusianus, a son of Tsar John Vladislav, who managed to escape from Constanti-nople, was proclaimed co-ruler the insurrection spread throughout the Balkans and northern Greece. Lack of unity among the leaders of this revolt led to its collapse in 1041, after the treacherous Alusianus had enticed Peter Delyan to a banquet and there gouged out his eyes in an ambush.

The second half of the eleventh century was marked by a steady decline in internal security in Bulgaria and the Balkans. The Hungarians attacked the Byzantine Empire from the north, and in 1064 they seized Belgrade. A swarming horde of Tatar nomads, akin to the Pechenegs and known as the Uzes, left the steppes of South Russia and poured through Moldavia into the Balkans in the autumn of 1064. Bulgarian territory, including Macedonia and Thrace as well as northern Greece, was ravaged by these savage invaders. However, a devastating plague, hailed by the pious as a miracle, rid the Empire of most of the Uzes; the survivors either fled across the Danube, or entered the Byzantine service. DISORDERS
IN THE
BALKANS

The year 1071 brought fresh disasters to Byzantium. In that year, Bari in Italy fell into the hands of the Normans under Robert Guiscard, while to the east in farthest Armenia, the imperial army commanded by Emperor Romanus was annihilated by the Turks, and Romanus himself captured. Released the following year, he was blinded by his rivals and died before the year was out. Asia Minor, from which derived so much of the strength of the Byzantine armies, was largely overrun by the Seljuq Turks.

All this encouraged insurgents in the Balkans. In 1072, a fresh revolt broke out in the territories which had once formed the nucleus of Tsar Samuel's domains. The rebels were supported by the principality of Zeta, on the Adriatic; Constantine Bodin, the son of Prince Michael of Zeta, was crowned Tsar in Prizren. In Bulgaria proper, the standard of revolt was raised by the boyar Georgi Voiteh.

Although this revolt was soon crushed, fresh unrest broke out in Bulgaria in 1074, 1079, and again in 1084.

The troubled internal situation was exploited increasingly by the Bogomils (see next chapter), one of whose strongholds was Plovdiv, the metropolis of Thrace. Here Slavs and Greeks lived side by side with numerous Armenians, who had long since introduced their own national brand of religious heresy, a form of Paulicianism. Partly to combat these heretics the Byzantine 'Grand Domestic' or Commander-in-chief in the West, an Armenian adherent of the Georgian Orthodox faith, Gregory Bakuriani or Pacurianos by name, built the magnificent monastery of Bachkovo, south of Assenovgrad (1083). This monastery was placed in the hands of Georgian monks, though later taken over by Greeks and then by Bulgarians. As for the Bogomils and Paulicians, the outstanding Byzantine emperor Alexius Comnenus (1081–1118) devoted much energy to largely fruitless attempts to convert or suppress them, as we read in the *Alexiad*, a biography written by the emperor's daughter, Princess Anna Comnena. Many of these Bogomils endured agonizing tortures, or chose to be burnt alive, rather than abandon their beliefs.

Plate 28

ARRIVAL OF THE CRUSADERS

At the end of the eleventh century, fresh trouble beset the hapless Bulgarians, in the shape of the disorderly hordes of Westerners who passed through the Balkans in the course of the First Crusade in 1096. Their leader was Peter the Hermit, who regarded the Orthodox Bulgarians as heretics, and did nothing to stem the ensuing violence, pillage and arson. The same pattern was repeated at the time of the Second Crusade, in 1147. However, these injuries were to be amply repaid after Bulgaria regained her independence, as we shall see.

BULGARIA REGAINS INDEPEND-ENCE

There was little the Bulgarians could do but bide their time, and dream of freedom, as they recalled the heroic age of Tsars Symeon and Samuel. Their moment came in 1185, when the Sicilian Normans attacked the Byzantine possessions along the Adriatic and in Greece, capturing Durazzo (Dyrrachium), and Thessalonica. The last emperor of the Comnenus dynasty, Andronicus, was torn to pieces in Constantinople on 12 September 1185 by an enraged and panic-stricken mob.

The Comnenoi were succeeded by the Angelus dynasty, first in the person of Isaac II (1185–95), of whom it was said that he sold government jobs like vegetables in a market. No sooner had Isaac assumed the purple than he imposed heavy special taxes, on the occasion of his dynastic marriage with the ten-year-old daughter of the King of Hungary.

The Vlachs of the Balkans sent two of their number, the brothers Peter and Assen, to negotiate with Emperor Isaac. The brothers, who owned land and castles in the neighbourhood of Great Tărnovo, made

Fig. 11 *Medieval Bulgarian helmet styles. Left:
Detail from fresco at Dragalevtsi monastery, near Sofia;
right: Detail from fresco at St Theodore's church,
Boboshevo. (After Manova)*

certain requests for grants of feudal lands and privileges, which were curtly dismissed – a Byzantine courtier even slapping Assen in the face. The infuriated brothers rode swiftly back to Tărnovo. The news of their humiliation spread like wildfire. An uprising was proclaimed in one of the leading churches of the city on the Yantra; and insurrection was soon rife throughout northeastern Bulgaria. The rebellion spread into Thrace, and imperial troops sent to suppress it were three times defeated.

Emperor Isaac himself set out on campaign in 1186, and temporarily drove the insurgent Bulgarians and Vlachs beyond the Danube, into Wallachia. Soon they were back again with Cuman auxiliaries. After a vain attempt to besiege and capture Lovech, Isaac Angelus concluded peace, recognizing the autonomy of the brothers Peter and Assen, and taking with him as hostage a third brother of theirs, the future Bulgarian tsar Kaloyan.

Before long, however, many Bulgarian boyars came to envy Peter and Assen their royal status, and in 1196 the unrest that had been seething erupted. That year Assen was murdered by Ivanko, an ambitious nobleman, and his brother Peter suffered a similar fate a few months later.

The third of the ambitious brothers, Kaloyan, sometimes known as Ioannicius (Ioannitsa), now came into his own. Kaloyan, who reigned from 1197 to 1207, is a key figure in medieval Bulgarian history: his intervention in the struggle between Rome and the Crusaders on the one hand, and the Byzantine empire of Nicaea on the other, proved to be of decisive importance. Kaloyan was anxious to establish the legitimacy of his rule, and from 1199 kept up an interesting correspondence with Pope Innocent III, culminating in the sending of a papal legate, Bishop

TSAR
KALOYAN
THE BRAVE

75

John de Casemaris, from Rome to Tărnovo. On 7 November 1204, the Legate consecrated the Bulgarian Archbishop Basil as primate and patriarch of Bulgaria, and the next day placed the royal crown on Kaloyan's head.

However, Bulgarian relations with the Latins at this period were by no means uniformly cordial. The marauding activities of the Third Crusade passing through Bulgaria in 1189 were particularly resented. The Crusaders suspected the Byzantine emperor of instigating Bulgarian guerilla fighters. In a letter to his son and successor, Henry VI, Emperor Frederick Barbarossa reported that thirty-two Bulgarians had been hanged in a single day, 'suspended like wolves', and that their comrades had shadowed the Crusaders as far as Plovdiv, molesting them with nocturnal raids through all the Bulgarian forests. 'Yet our army in turn dreadfully tortured great numbers of them with various kinds of torments.'

Byzantium finally fell to the Crusaders in 1204, and Baldwin of Flanders set himself up as emperor. Tsar Kaloyan at first adopted a conciliatory policy towards the Latin Empire of Constantinople. How-ever, the Latins were haughty; they informed Kaloyan that the Balkans belonged to the Byzantine sphere of authority, and that they considered Kaloyan and his subjects to be their vassals. The Bulgarian tsar there-upon allied himself with various dissatisfied Greek nobles, and invaded Thrace. In a great battle, fought in 1205 near Adrianople, the Crusaders were decisively defeated. Emperor Baldwin was taken prisoner. Accord-ing to one account, he was imprisoned for life in the Baldwin Tower on the Tsarevets acropolis at Tărnovo. The Latin Empire never fully re-covered from this shattering blow; the Greeks were enabled to maintain the rival empire of Nicaea, which remained the leading stronghold of Greek culture and political power until the downfall of the Latin regime in Constantinople, in 1261.

Copying the example of the Byzantine emperor Basil the Bulgar-Slayer, Kaloyan styled himself 'the slayer of Romans'. In 1207 he marched westwards and rapidly conquered most of Macedonia. In September of that year, he ambushed and slew the Crusaders' leader Boniface of Montferrat. Two months later, as he was besieging Thes-salonica, Kaloyan was murdered in his tent by the Cuman Voivoda Manastras, a move instigated by dissident Bulgar boyars.

Fig. 12

Fig. 12 St Demetrius, patron saint of Thessalonica, slaying the Bulgarian Tsar Kaloyan (1207). Kaloyan was actually murdered while besieging that city, by the Voivoda Manastras; this was regarded as divine punishment. From a fourteenth-century Gospel miniature, in the Rila monastery. (After Naslednikova)

The boyars set on the throne a nephew of Kaloyan, Boril by name (1207–18). An unpopular and feeble ruler, Boril is chiefly remembered for the Church council which he summoned in 1211 to try and root out the Bogomil heresy. The Bogomils identified themselves with the oppressed and impoverished peasants and townsfolk, and enjoyed considerable popular support. Boril's persecutions, as well as his military ineptitude, led to a revolt in Vidin. In 1218, the son of Tsar Assen I, by name Ivan Assen, returned from exile in Russia at the head of a company of Russian and Cuman mercenaries, and also a Bulgarian contingent. The citizens of Tărnovo opened their gates to him; Tsar Boril was deposed and blinded, and Ivan Assen began his victorious and brilliant reign as tsar which lasted until 1241.

BORIL THE INEPT

Ivan Assen II rapidly restored the shattered fortunes of the Bulgarian realm. He himself married the daughter of the King of Hungary; one of his daughters he married to the brother of the Despot of Epirus, and a second to the son of the King of Serbia. The Latins in Constantinople invited Ivan Assen to marry his youngest daughter Elena to the youthful Emperor Baldwin II (1228–61), and to act as regent for Baldwin throughout his minority.

ACHIEVEMENTS OF TSAR IVAN ASSEN II

Fig. 13

The prospect of Bulgarian domination at Constantinople alarmed the ambitious Greek Despot of Epirus, Theodore Angelus (also referred to in the sources as Theodore Ducas and Theodore Comnenus, through his family connections with these great Houses). Theodore denounced his former alliance with Bulgaria and in 1230 invaded Thrace from Adrianople. Tsar Ivan Assen II marched out to meet the invaders with a banner to which he attached the actual parchment of the treaty which Theodore had violated. A pitched battle took place close to the village of Klokotnitsa, near Haskovo, on the day of the Forty Martyrs. The Greek and other levies of Theodore Angelus were annihilated or put to flight, and the Despot himself was captured and blinded.

In memory of this victory, Ivan Assen II built and dedicated the church of the Forty Martyrs by a bridge at the foot of the Tsarevets acropolis in Tărnovo. As well as installing there the fine inscribed granite pillar of the old Bulgar Khan Omurtag, he set up a commemorative marble column of his own recording the victory at Klokotnitsa, and

Fig. 13 Bulgaria and the Latin States after the fall of Constantinople in 1204, showing the location of the Battle of Klokotnitsa (1230)

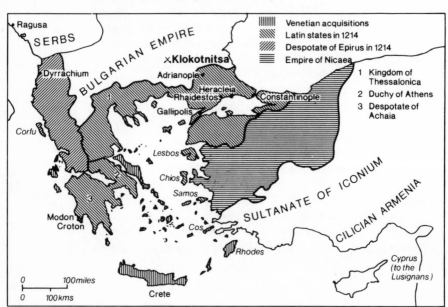

Fig. 14 A Bulgarian tsar (Ivan Assen II?) and his warriors. Scene commemorating the Battle of Klokotnitsa, from a fourteenth-century fresco painting in the church of Saints Peter and Paul, Great Tărnovo. (After Naslednikova)

declaring himself lord of all territories from Adrianople to Durazzo – Greek, Serbian and Albanian alike:

> The Franks hold only the cities close to Constantinople and Constantinople itself; but even they are under the sway of my empire, since they have no other Tsar but me, and only thanks to me do they survive, for God has so ordained it.

Another notable success of this outstanding monarch was the final restoration of the Bulgarian Orthodox patriarchate, initiated by Kaloyan, but under Papal sponsorship, in 1204. This time, the Greek Orthodox bishops of Nicaea recognized Joachim, the Bulgarian Metropolitan of Tărnovo, as an autonomous patriarch, in 1235. The Bulgarian patriarchate endured until the fall of Tărnovo to the Turks in 1393, and was then extinguished until after the liberation of Bulgaria in 1877–78.

The name of Tsar Ivan Assen is closely linked to the part of the Rhodope fortress system which lies astride the main road from Plovdiv southwards over the mountains to the Aegean, via the modern Smolyan region. Immediately south of Assenovgrad ('city of Assen') is the craggy and inaccessible Assenova Krepost or Assen's Castle, with its distinctive

Plate 29

Fig. 37

church of the Virgin of Petrich. This complex of buildings was restored by Ivan Assen in 1231, and used as a fortress until 1410. On the cliff is a little known Slavonic inscription, the gist of which is:

> In the year 6739 from the Creation [1231], Indiction 4, the man elevated by God, Ivan Assen II, tsar of the Bulgarians, Greeks and other peoples, fortified this castle, and installed as governor of the fortress Alexis the Sebastos ('Sevast').

It is interesting to note that the wording of this inscription so offended certain local Greeks that the original text was effaced in 1883 by order of the mayor of Assenovgrad. Fortunately it had been recorded earlier, and could be restored by the initiative of the historian Professor V. N. Zlatarski. I saw and verified the renewed inscription when I visited Assen's Castle in 1971.

This mention of an official bearing the exalted title of *sebastos* reminds us of the extent to which the state and court apparatus of the Second Bulgarian Empire was impregnated with Byzantine elements. Medieval manuscripts and frescoes show us Bulgarian rulers, princes and prin‑

Fig. 15

cesses clad in exact replicas of Byzantine robes and regalia. In Bulgarian charters we find mention of dignitaries termed *comes* ('count'); *kefaliya* or

Fig. 15 Bulgarian provincial grandee: Constantine, Despot of Kyustendil, with his wife, Tamara, daughter of Tsar Ivan Alexander, and two of her sisters. In the painting, the court costumes shine with scarlet and gold, making it one of the finest Bulgarian medieval family portrait groups. From the fourteenth‑century Gospel manuscript of Tsar Ivan Alexander, in the British Library. (After Naslednikova)

Fig. 16 Great Tărnovo in the fourteenth century. Architect's reconstruction. (After B. Kuzupov)

kephalotes, a chief or headman; *duka* or duke; *kastrophylax* or castle commandant; *epikerni*, originally a wine-taster, later a privy councillor; *catepan*, a military governor-general: *alagator*, a squadron commander, and many others. There are also a number of purely Slavonic titles. Gone for ever are the old Bulgar ranks of *tarkhan*, *bagatur* and so many others, thus indicating that the tsars of the Second Bulgarian Empire had repudiated their old nomadic Turkic past and had been drawn into the cultural orbit of Constantinople.

Fiscal terms of this period relating to taxes and dues are often derived from Byzantine originals, as evinced by such Bulgarian words as *komod*, *mitat* and *ariko*. (*Mitaton* in Greek means a tax or tax office, *aerikon* is the poll-tax.)

Tsar Ivan Assen II reorganized the financial system of Bulgaria, being the first ruler to strike coinage in large quantities, mostly silver pieces (aspers). The coinage was partly modelled on that of Venice, with

Plate 55

which power the Tărnovo court did a great amount of business. Affini⸗ ties also exist between the Bulgarian silver coinage and that of the Greek empire of Trebizond, the Trebizond asper or 'white piece', also the silver coinage of Cilician Armenia. Beautiful gold pieces were struck, resembling the Byzantine *scyphate* or concave *nomisma*.

A network of roads – though most of them were little better than tracks – linked Tărnovo with Durazzo and Ragusa (Dubrovnik) on the Adriatic, and Varna, Nessebăr and Burgas on the Black Sea. Another highway led over the modern Shipka Pass towards Adrianople and Constantinople. The journey from Tărnovo to Durazzo via Lovech, Sofia and Kyustendil commonly took as long as thirty days.

A substantial merchant quarter existed at the foot of the Tărnovo acropolis of Tsarevets, largely inhabited by foreign business men and their families and staff – rather like the Moscow foreigners' *sloboda* of the sixteenth and seventeenth centuries. Now a suburb of modern Tărnovo, the site of this medieval merchant quarter was pointed out to me when I visited the city in 1967 and 1971. According to documents published by F. Miklosich and others, Ivan Assen II showed special favour to the Ragusans, merchants from Dubrovnik, since these were largely Slav by blood. He granted them numerous privileges and styled them his 'well⸗ beloved and most faithful guests'.

Fig. 16

DECLINE OF THE CENTRAL POWER

After the death of Ivan Assen II in 1241, decline set in. External dangers – particularly the onslaughts of the Mongols – and rapid changes of ruler at home led to scenes of violence. In the space of four decades, Bulgaria had six rulers: Koloman I (1241–46), Michael II Assen (1246–57), the usurper Mico (1257), then Constantine Assen Tikh the cripple (1257–77), the swineherd Ivailo (1277–79), and Ivan Assen III (1279–80). John III Vatatzes, emperor of Nicaea (d. 1254), took the offensive against Michael II Assen, and recaptured the Rhodope region, Adrianople and other parts of southern Bulgaria, while Michael VIII Palaeologus extended the Byzantine frontier to the foot⸗hills of the Balkan range, and seized the Black Sea ports of Sozopol, Develtus, Anchialus and Nessebăr (1263).

Plates 30–32

Plate 33

The Hungarians captured Vidin on the Danube, which from 1261 became the centre of an autonomous West Bulgarian province, ruled by a vassal of Hungary named Yakov Svetoslav, who arrogated to himself

Fig. 17 Tsar Constantine Assen Tikh and Empress Irina. Fresco in the Boyana church, near Sofia (1259). The tsar, portrayed in his prime, wears the regalia of the Bulgarian court, modelled on that of Byzantium; in later years he became a cripple. (After Naslednikova)

the title of tsar. After the death of the Hungarian king Stephen V in 1272, Svetoslav ruled for some years as a virtually independent sovereign.

The twenty-year reign of Constantine Assen Tikh was marked by a deterioration in the lot of the common people. To maintain himself in power, the cripple Constantine married a Byzantine princess, paid tribute to the Tatar Khan of the Golden Horde, and turned a blind eye to the exactions of the boyars and of the established Church. All this weighed down on the peasantry, burdened as they were with dues in kind and in cash, with forced labour and corvees, also military service at the beck and call of their feudal lord and of their king. Bogomil propaganda continued, preaching a nihilistic and anarchistic attitude towards Church and State.

KING IVAILO
THE
SWINEHERD

The result of all this was the uprising of the swineherd Ivailo in 1277. Few episodes in Bulgarian history can rival this amazing saga, which resulted in a simple peasant being crowned Tsar in Great Tărnovo. Many features of the uprising anticipate the rebellions of Wat Tyler and Robert Ket in fourteenth- and sixteenth-century England and those of Stenka Razin and Pugachev in seventeenth- and eighteenth-century Russia.

The Bulgarians

According to the Byzantine chronicler Pachymeres (1242–1310), Ivailo was a simple peasant of austere habits who fed on bread and wild berries. In conversation with other peasants as poor as himself, Ivailo would often tell of strange visions of his mysterious destiny, which, he was convinced, was to save Bulgaria from her plight, and regenerate the nation. Ivailo began by gathering around him a band of determined patriots who attacked local detachments of the Mongol Golden Horde, and hurled them back across the Danube. Advancing on Tărnovo, Ivailo was met by the royal army of Tsar Constantine Assen Tikh, who was defeated and slain on the battlefield. The whole of Bulgaria rapidly fell under Ivailo's sway, and events culminated in his marriage to the Empress Maria, a Greek princess, and widow of the slain Tsar Constantine Assen Tikh.

Within two years, the régime of the swineherd tsar Ivailo was brought to an abrupt end. The simple peasants who had supported him grew disillusioned with his royal pretensions and excessive pride; the Byzantines sent an expeditionary force with a protégé of Constantinople, who was installed on the throne of Tărnovo as Ivan Assen III (1279–80). Ivailo put Ivan Assen III to flight, only to find himself assailed by the feudal nobles, who proclaimed one of their number, George Terter, tsar. Ivailo attempted to enlist the support of the Tatars to restore his fortunes, but he was assassinated at a banquet by orders of the Mongol khan Nogai.

THE RISE OF
SERBIA

The continuing weakness of the Bulgarian state contributed to a most important phenomenon in Balkan history of the thirteenth and fourteenth centuries – namely the rise of Serbia under the Nemanya dynasty. The founder of the dynasty in 1168 was Stephen Nemanya, Grand Zhupan of Rashka. Stephen's youngest son, Prince Rastko, secretly left his father's court and went to Mount Athos to become a monk. Under the name of Sava, Rastko became the first archbishop of Serbia, a patron of education and one of the country's eminent statesmen. St Sava was a friend of the Bulgarian tsar Ivan Assen II, and died at Tărnovo while on a pastoral mission to Bulgaria. He is buried there in the church of the Forty Martyrs, at the foot of the Tsarevets palace hill.

Other distinguished members of the Serbian Nemanya dynasty were Stephen Urosh I (1243–76), and his son Milutin (1281–1321), Stephen

Urosh III Dechanski (1321–31), and Stephen Dushan (1331–55). It was Stephen Dechanski who slew the Bulgarian tsar Michael Shish-man at Kyustendil in 1330; Dushan took Ohrida, Salonica and Mount Athos, and revived the idea of a Slav emperor of Byzantium, an idea which had been so dear to the Bulgarian tsar Symeon, and had been briefly taken up by Ivan Assen II. The growing political and cultural might of Serbia was certainly a contributory cause of the relative decline of Bulgaria after the 'proletarian interlude' associated with the name of the peasant tsar Ivailo.

Tsar George Terter (1280–92) is often considered to have been of Cuman descent. He embarked on a strongly anti-Byzantine foreign policy, allying himself with Charles of Anjou, ruler of Sicily, who was planning an all-out onslaught on the newly restored Byzantine Empire. The famous uprising known as the Sicilian Vespers took place in 1282, and put paid to Charles of Anjou's military plans and dreams of empire. The uprising also resulted in a strengthening of the Byzantine position in the Adriatic and the Balkans, and in an invasion of Bulgaria by the Mongol khan Nogai, with whom the Byzantine emperor Michael VIII had struck up an alliance. Tsar George Terter was even forced to submit to becoming a Tatar vassal. In the West, an autonomous state arose under the despot Shishman, with its capital at Vidin. Shishman was to be the founding father of Bulgaria's last royal dynasty of medieval times, the Shishmanids.

GEORGE TERTER AND HIS SUCCESSORS

Tsar George Terter finally fled the country and took refuge in Byzan-tium. The Mongol Nogai set up as tsar a minor bolyar, Smilets by name, who reigned from 1292 to 1298. However, he was displaced by the young and vigorous son of Tsar George Terter, Theodore Svetoslav, who eliminated the Mongol element root and branch. Patriarch Joachim II, accused of unduly favouring the Mongols, was sentenced to summary execution by being hurled off a high crag on the Tsarevets in Tărnovo. This crag, which is still shown to visitors at the present day, was the 'Tarpeian Rock' of medieval Bulgaria, many alleged traitors and criminals meeting their doom there.

Theodore Svetoslav reigned for nearly a quarter of a century until 1322, and married Theodora, daughter of the Byzantine emperor. Taking advantage of the decline of the Byzantine Empire, he recovered

The Bulgarians

large tracts of Bulgarian territory south of the main Balkan range, includ, ing the Black Sea ports of Mesembria (Nessebăr), Sozopol and Anchi, alus. Through the towns of the Black Sea littoral, trade flourished with Venice and Genoa, and distinctive Bulgarian silver coins were struck in large numbers. The major article of export was grain, and the Genoese were important middlemen in provisioning the city of Con, stantinople with this vital commodity.

Plate 55

With the one, year reign of Theodore Svetoslav's son and successor, George II, the Terter dynasty became extinct.

THE
SHISHMAN
DYNASTY

The bolyars then elected as their tsar the Despot of Vidin, Michael Shishman, who reigned from 1323 until his death in battle against the Serbs in 1330. The Shishman dynasty is associated with the last flower, ing of Bulgaria's medieval culture prior to the Turkish onslaught, its members being great patrons of the arts and letters.

Plate 33

The reunion of Vidin, with its palace castle of Baba Vida, and the Tărnovo kingdom was an event of some moment. However, this had the effect of alienating Serbia, which had pretensions to suzerainty over Vidin. Michael Shishman was married to Anna, sister of the Serbian king Stephen Urosh III, whom he divorced in order to marry Theo, dora, sister of the Byzantine emperor Andronicus III. The Bulgarians were joined by the Byzantines for a military offensive against Serbia – a symbolic prelude to the disastrous Balkan Wars that became a feature of the European political scene just before World War I.

The Bulgarian attack on the Serbs in 1330 failed ignominiously with a military débacle at Velbuzhd (Kyustendil), in which Tsar Michael Shishman lost his life. The sole gainers from this affair were the Ottoman Turks, now established throughout much of Western Asia Minor and the Aegean littoral, and only waiting for the signal to invade the Balkans *en masse*, as they did with overwhelming success during the second half of the fourteenth century.

IVAN
ALEXANDER,
PATRON OF
THE ARTS

After a brief interlude, Michael Shishman's nephew Ivan Alexander was proclaimed tsar. The likeness of this interesting ruler may be seen in a large miniature painting in the Slavonic Gospel manuscript brought back from Mount Athos in 1837 by Robert Curzon (see Chapter VII); his family are also shown, in full regalia.

Fig. 18 Bronze coin of Tsar Michael Shishman (1323–30), found at Great Tărnovo. Obverse shows a crowned two-headed eagle; reverse, a cross upon an acanthus leaf. Diameter 18 mm. (After Nikola Angelov)

Ivan Alexander began his reign with a campaign against the Byzantine Empire. A decisive victory over the Greeks at Russocastro in 1332 enabled the Bulgarians to regain the Thracian lands which Emperor Andronicus III had seized after the battle of Velbuzhd two years before. A peace treaty was signed, and this peace lasted for thirty years. Tsar Ivan Alexander also improved relations with the King of Serbia.

In retrospect, the forty-year rule of Ivan Alexander appears as a false dawn, a swan-song of medieval Bulgaria's political and cultural glory. Yet the long reign had a favourable effect on its economic and cultural life. The home market and trade with the Byzantine Empire and with Venice revived. Bulgaria became a vital supplier of cereals and lumber, because the Turks had seized a large part of Asia Minor and cut off Constantinople's supplies of raw materials from the south and east; they had also interrupted the Egyptian trade with Venice. The Bulgarian Black Sea ports became animated centres of export and import trade. Nessebăr in particular was enriched by many new churches, public buildings and port installations, and a Venetian colony was set up in Varna.

Plates 30–32,
Fig. 38

Fig. 19 Tsar Ivan Alexander and his second consort, Empress Sara-Theodora, a converted Jewess, with two of their children: the future Tsar Ivan Shishman, and the Sebastocrator Ivan-Assen. From the Gospels of Tsar Ivan Alexander, in the British Library. (After Naslednikova)

87

Concerning Bulgarian relations with Venice a number of characteristic documents have come down to us. For instance, we learn that in 1352, Doge Andrea Dandolo sent an embassy to Tsar Ivan Alexander in Tărnovo, to negotiate a fresh trade treaty. This was signed on 4 October 1352, and includes several interesting features. Thus, the possessions of Venetian citizens are guaranteed against plunder or seizure in the event of shipwreck or death. In the event of an offence being committed by one member of the Venetian community, the other members are not to be held collectively responsible, nor for each other's debts. The houses of Venetians were immune from arbitrary entry or search. The Venetians had the right to build churches and trading depots anywhere they wished, even in the interior hinterland of the country. Customs duties were fixed at three per cent. These arrangements entailed a certain abrogation of Bulgarian suzerainty, and the Venetians gained advantages similar to those enjoyed by foreign powers in the Ottoman Empire, during the Capitulations.

Ivan Alexander was a great patron of the arts and sciences. The Tărnovo school of painting attained great renown; Slavonic manuscripts were copied and illuminated; new churches built, old ones restored and renovated. At the Kilifarevo monastery, not far from Tărnovo, a veritable Bulgarian academy was established by the monk Theodosius (see Chapter VI).

Plates 48–50

Fig. 20 Gold ear-rings, as worn by Bulgarian aristocratic ladies of the fourteenth century. (After Naslednikova)

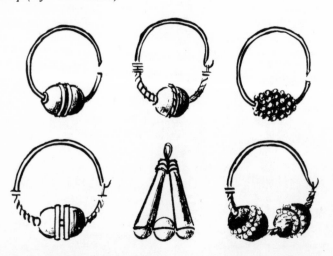

Fig. 21 Bronze coin showing Tsar Ivan Alexander with Empress Theodora (1355–71), found at Great Tărnovo. Reverse shows the royal monograms. Diameter 17 mm (After Nikola Angelov)

These improvements brought benefit mainly to the princely, the merchant and the monastic classes. The condition of the peasants and the urban poor failed to improve – indeed it grew worse. The peasants were the worst off, due to the intensification of serfdom, which bound them to the land, and inflicted crippling dues and taxes in cash and in kind. From the middle of the fourteenth century, hordes of Turks began to ravage the country, plundering and burning the villages, and carrying off the inhabitants to be sold as slaves. In despair, many of the serfs took to the hills and the Bulgarian lands became more and more depopulated.

A number of other factors combined to speed Bulgaria's decline in the DECLINE AND
later years of Ivan Alexander's reign. DECAY

Bogomilism once more reared its head, and other sects also appeared, such as the Adamites and the Varlaamites. Two Church councils held in Tărnovo, in 1350 and 1360, failed to put a stop to the ideological schism. Division within the Church was aggravated further by the spread of a quietist, contemplative doctrine known as Hesychasm, whose adepts are sometimes termed *umbilis animi* – people with their souls in their navels. This movement, whose supporters even included the Bulgarian patriarch Euthymius, was ill-fitted for this time of crisis, when Christianity in Byzantium and the Balkans was threatened by militant Islam.

Tsar Ivan Alexander himself contributed to the break-up of the *Fig. 21*
Bulgarian realm. He abandoned his first wife, and married Theodora, a converted Jewess. The doting monarch disinherited the sons of his first marriage, to proclaim as heir his son by Theodora, Ivan Shishman. In order to placate the rightful heir, his eldest son Ivan Stratsimir, the tsar separated off Vidin from the Bulgarian monarchy about 1360, and set up Stratsimir as ruler there. From 1365 to 1370, Vidin was occupied by the Hungarians, who sent Franciscan monks to convert the people to the Roman faith.

The Bulgarians

The boyar Balik set himself up as an independent ruler in the Dobrudja; he was succeeded by his brother Dobroditsa (from whose name that of the region derives).

All this contributed to the rapid spread of Turkish power in the Balkans. In 1362, Adrianople fell to the Turks, thus blocking the land route from Bulgaria to Constantinople. Two years later, general Lala Shahin entered Plovdiv, and took up his residence there as the first Turkish *beylerbeyi* of Rumelia, as the region was to be called for the next five centuries. Sultan Murad I (1362–89) established his court at Adrianople. The Turkish advance was accompanied by systematic measures for colonization. The native population was removed in great numbers to slavery in Asia Minor. Turkish colonists were settled in the conquered districts, and the Ottoman nobles, especially the Sultan's generals, were rewarded with generous gifts of land. On the Black Sea, the Byzantines took the opportunity in 1364 of reoccupying the port of Anchialus, north of the bay of Burgas. Amadeus of Savoy took Nessebăr from Ivan Alexander in 1366, and handed it over to his cousin, the Byzantine emperor John V Palaeologus.

THE END OF THE BULGARIAN EMPIRE
The last of the Shishman dynasty, Ivan (1371–93), inherited a virtually impossible task, and acquitted himself gallantly up to the inevitable débâcle. Ivan Shishman's reign began most inauspiciously. The Serbs attempted to check the Ottoman advance into Macedonia, and this culminated in the battle of Chernomen, on the river Maritsa, which took place in September 1371. Drunk with wine and conceit, the large Serbian army was surprised by a handful of Turkish Spahis, and annihilated together with its commanders.

During the following months, many Bulgarian towns fell to the Turks. These included Yambol, Karnobat and Samokov, though the great centre of Sredets, the modern Sofia, held out until 1385. Both the Byzantine emperor John V Palaeologus, and the Bulgarian tsar, were forced to bow the knee before Sultan Murad, and acknowledge themselves his vassals. Ivan Shishman sent his beautiful sister, Kera-Tamara, to the Sultan's harem.

Fig. 22 Bronze coin of Tsar Ivan Shishman (1371–93), found at Great Tărnovo. Obverse shows royal monogram; reverse, a lion rampant. Diameter 20 mm. (After Nikola Angelov)

All this encouraged the rulers of the breakaway Bulgarian states of Vidin and of the Dobrudja in their centrifugal aims and ambitions. Ivan Shishman's half-brother, Ivan Stratsimir, advanced southwards from his capital at Vidin, and invaded the Sofia plain. In the Dobrudja the despot Dobroditsa also remained independent of the Bulgarian tsar in Tărnovo. He contrived to construct a fleet of his own, with which he fought the Genoese; he even sent a naval force right across the Black Sea to intervene in the internal disputes of the empire of Trebizond. When Dobroditsa's son, Ivanko, succeeded him, he reversed his father's policy and concluded a commercial pact with Genoa in 1387.

A last flicker of Bulgarian national resistance occurred in 1387. In that year, Prince Lazar of Serbia and Tvurdko, Ban of Bosnia, defeated the Turks at Plochnik. Tsar Ivan Shishman threw off the Turkish yoke and installed himself in the fortified castle of Nicopolis on the Danube. The despatch of an Ottoman force thirty thousand strong soon brought him to heel. A number of Bulgarian strong-points were occupied by the Turks, as a prelude to the final annexation of the land. For instance, the impregnable castle of Ovechgrad above Provadia (between Tărnovo and Varna) was occupied by a ruse in 1388, when a Turkish expeditionary force under 'Alī Pasha pleaded with the Bulgarian commandant for shelter from the bad weather. The Turks, characteristically enough, rose in a body during the night, murdered their Bulgarian hosts, and took over the fortress. These and many other interesting details were related to me when I visited Provadia in 1971 in company with Mr Alexander Kuzov of the Varna Archaeological Museum.

The Balkan Christians suffered a fresh disaster at the battle of Kossovo Field ('the field of the Blackbirds') on 15 June 1389, in which Prince Lazar's Serbian and allied troops were overwhelmed by the Ottomans. Sultan Murad was killed by a Serbian patriot, but the Serbs and Bosnians were cut to pieces by the Turks. Prince Lazar was taken prisoner and executed together with his nobles.

The new sultan, Bayazid, lost no time in completing his conquest of what remained of independent Bulgaria. After a three-month siege, in which the townsfolk were led and inspired by Patriarch Euthymius, Great Tărnovo fell on 17 July 1393. Euthymius was imprisoned in a monastery, and both the independent Bulgarian patriarchate and the Shishman dynasty were brought to an end.

Fig. 16

The autonomous provinces of the Dobrudja and Vidin were soon swallowed up by the Turkish sultan. In the Dobrudja, the despot Ivanko was replaced for a short period (1390–91) by the Wallachian prince from southern Romania, Voivode Mircea the Old; but after this short interlude the Dobrudja fell to the Turks. Tsar Ivan Stratsimir ruled for a short time in Vidin on the Danube, as a Turkish vassal.

The final collapse of Christian hopes for the liberation of the Balkans occurred in 1396. The occupation of Bulgaria meant that Catholic Hungary was directly threatened, while the Latin principalities in and around Greece felt themselves menaced. The Pope and the Venetians spurred on King Sigismund of Hungary to undertake a crusade against the infidel; this was joined by a contingent of knights from France, while Venice despatched a small fleet to the Dardanelles. But the motley army of King Sigismund and his Western allies had scarcely crossed the Danube when they were annihilated by a well disciplined Turkish army which fell upon them near Nicopolis, on 25 September 1396.

The last surviving Bulgarian dynast, Ivan Stratsimir, had allowed the Crusaders free passage through Vidin on their way from Hungary. Sultan Bayazid now took over Vidin and deposed Stratsimir. With him there perished the last vestiges of Bulgarian independence, which was to lie submerged until the war of liberation in 1877, nearly five centuries later. It is, however, worth noting that sporadic attempts by Western Christendom to liberate the Balkans and free Byzantium from the Turk' ish yoke continued right up to the middle of the fifteenth century. It was on Bulgarian territory, near Varna, on 10 November 1444, that the great battle took place which ended in an Ottoman victory, and the death of Vladislav III, King of Hungary and Poland. Cardinal Cesarini, the instigator of this belated and unfortunate Crusade, also lost his life. All this in turn led to the isolation, and then, the capture of Constantinople in 1453.

CHAPTER V

Social Protest: The Bogomil Heresy

In the preceding historical chapters, there are references to a medieval heresy known as Bogomilism. We must now attempt to relate this movement to the Bulgarian social background of those times, and also to general currents of religious thought in the Middle Ages.

By the reign of Tsar Peter (927–69), Bulgaria was ripe for heresy and revolt. The conversion of Bulgaria to Christianity by Prince Boris-Michael in 865 had led to wide-spread popular discontent. Cherished pagan customs had been brutally suppressed. Things got worse for the Bulgarian masses under Tsar Symeon, who adorned Preslav with expensive palaces, and indulged in ruinous wars.

ORIGINS OF BOGOMILISM

The presence of many Paulicians in the Balkans, as witnessed by such place names as Pavlikeni, a market town between Tărnovo and Levski, provided an ideological rallying-point for religious and political opposition to Church and State. There was always the possibility that the Paulicians, mainly Armenians and Greeks, would gradually die out as a sect, and that their ideas would remain alien and inaccessible to the local Slavs. The importance of the priest Bogomil lies in the fact that he succeeded in drawing together the strands of earlier heresies, including those of the Paulicians, the Massalians, the Marcionites and the Manichaeans, and wove them into a fabric of moral and political teaching adapted to the tastes and understanding of the simple Bulgarian peasantry and townsfolk. In doing so, Bogomil cleverly added a number of original features of a specifically Bulgarian popular flavour.

We know that Bogomil's heresy was well-established in Bulgaria by the year 950, because about this time Tsar Peter addressed two epistles to the patriarch Theophylact of Constantinople, who was the uncle of the tsaritsa Maria-Irene of Bulgaria. Peter expressed great concern about the virulent anti-clerical movement that had sprung up in the land, and Theophylact sent back a catechism to apply to the heretics, and advice on how to stamp out the movement by exercise of tact and diplomacy.

Fig. 23 Bulgarian pagans slaying Christians. Such scenes occurred throughout the ninth century. Pagan opposition to the Orthodox Church contributed later to the spread of Bogomilism. Miniature from the Menologium of Byzantine Emperor Basil II, in the Vatican Library. (After Naslednikova)

Some years later, around 970, an indignant Bulgarian priest named Cosmas composed a discourse against the Bogomils. Cosmas also took this opportunity to denounce the laziness and luxury of the Orthodox Church hierarchy, which contributed to the Bogomils' success.

BOGOMIL VIEW OF THE UNIVERSE

Our knowledge of Bogomil philosophy is largely derived from the polemical writings of their enemies, such as Cosmas, and the Byzantine theologian Euthymius Zigabenus. There is also a Bogomil apocryphon called *The Gospel of John*, or *The Secret Book*.

The Bogomil view of the nature of God and the world was akin to dualism, if not in its absolute form. The Bogomils held that Satan had not always been the Prince of Evil. God had originally reigned alone over a spiritual universe. The Trinity existed in Him: the Son and the Holy Ghost were emanations, which later took on a separate form. They were sent forth by God to cope with the problems of the material created world: when this world is eventually liquidated, they will resolve back into Him.

According to the Bogomils, the Father begat the Son, and the Son begat the Holy Ghost. The Holy Ghost begat the Twelve Apostles, including Judas. Satan was also a son of God the Father: he was in fact the first-born, and called Satanael, the suffix 'el' indicating his divine nature. Satanael was the steward of Heaven. God created a vast universe, composed of seven heavens and four fundamental elements: fire, water, air and earth. Satanael helped to administer this universe, but his real ambition was to become God's equal, and to set up his throne in the Seventh Heaven. He won over part of the angel host to help him to achieve his aims by such a plot. But the plot failed, and Satanael and the rebel angels were cast forth from Heaven.

The Bogomils liked to quote the words of the Prophet Isaiah (xiv, 12–15):

How art thou fallen from heaven, O Lucifer, son of the morning! how art thou cut down to the ground, which didst weaken the nations!

For thou hast said in thine heart, I will ascend into heaven, I will exalt my throne above the stars of God: I will sit also upon the mount of the congregation, in the sides of the north:

I will ascend above the heights of the clouds;

I will be like the most High.

Yet thou shalt be brought down to hell, to the sides of the pit . . .

Even after this defeat, the Bogomils believed, Satan retained his creative power, and began to reconstruct the world and build his own kingdom on earth. Satanael created the seas and oceans, made stars and planets, and fashioned plants and animals. In the end, to people his dominion, he made Adam out of earth and water. But Satan could only make a physical body for Adam, and failed in his attempt to breathe his spirit into Adam's inert frame. So Satan sent an embassy to God the Father to ask for a little life for Adam, promising that man, thus brought to life, should be shared between them. So God breathed His spirit into Adam, and the process was later repeated for Eve.

Adam was allowed to till the earth, on condition that he sold himself and his posterity to the Devil, the owner of the earth. But as a result of an appeal by the souls of a few elect men, God sent His Son, the Word, who is the same as the Archangel Michael, to go down into the world as Jesus Christ, to cure all ills. Jesus entered the Holy Virgin Mary through her ear, took flesh there and emerged by the same route.

Through Satanael's machinations, the Crucifixion took place. However, by seeming to die, Jesus was able to descend into Hell, bind Satanael, and take the divine suffix 'el' away from his name. Henceforth, he was simply Satan, the Devil. Satan was the inventor of the entire Orthodox community, with its churches and cathedrals, vestments and ceremonies, sacraments and fasts, and its complements of bishops, monks and priests.

This state of things would not last for ever. After Christ's Second Coming, said the Bogomils, Satan and his accomplices would be thrown out of the world altogether and sink down into Hell. All agents of earthly oppression and Church pomp would follow Satan there. But the righteous, who believed in and followed the Bogomil doctrine, would go to Heaven and live in eternal bliss.

BOGOMIL
DOCTRINE
AND
MORALITY

Logically enough, the Bogomils denounced the Orthodox Church, and rejected a large part of Holy Scripture, especially most of the Old Testament. They admitted the New Testament, the Psalms of David, and the Prophets; obviously, they had to reject the account of Creation given in Genesis. Like the Paulicians, the Bogomils detested the Cross as the instrument of Christ's torture by the Devil. They considered churches as abodes of demons; these were to be respected and humoured, lest they harm the faithful. (This quaint idea is thought by the Byzantine writer Euthymius Zigabenus to derive from the Massalians.) Church baptism and communion were rejected by the Bogomils. John the Baptist was even stigmatized as a servant of the Devil.

The Bogomils based their morality, as the Manichaeans had always done, on the view that the visible world was inherently evil, and that salvation could only lie in deliberate withdrawal from it. To some extent, this view was similar to the ideology of medieval monasticism. It is no coincidence that the story of Barlaam and Josaphat, which is based on the Great Renunciation of Gautama Buddha, became popular at an early date among the Manichees of Central Asia, spread to the Baghdad of Harun al-Rashid, was then taken over by the Christian Georgians and the Byzantine Greeks. Sometime in the eleventh century or later, the Barlaam and Josaphat story found its way into the Old Slavonic literature of Bulgaria. Both the Bogomils and the Bulgarian Orthodox found much to interest them in this Christianized Manichaean tract, which enjoins that renunciation of all the pleasures of the flesh, including wealth, rich food and sexual intercourse, is the only way to throw off man's carnal, wicked nature, and draw nearer to the divine, spiritual essence.

Only the Bogomil 'Elect' were expected to subject themselves to the full rigour of the Bogomil ethic, though the 'Simple Believers' and 'Hearers', both male and female, could graduate in time to the highest rank. Their enemies fabricated many calumnies against them, including the familiar charge of homosexuality. This charge, levelled against the Bulgarian Bogomils, in turn gave rise to the opprobrious epithet 'bougre', a derivation from the word 'Bulgar' – though the Bulgarians as a whole have always been noted for a healthy and normal hetero‑sexual attitude to life.

Cosmas the priest asserts that in outward appearance, the Bogomils were 'lamb‑like, gentle, modest and silent, and pale from hypocritical fasting'. They lived a retired life, masquerading as Orthodox Christians, to avoid falling victim to persecution. 'They do not talk idly,' Cosmas adds, 'nor laugh loudly, nor give themselves airs.' However, the Bogomil Elect encouraged simple peasants to ask them for spiritual guidance, thereby providing an opportunity to 'sow the tares of their teaching, blaspheming the tradition and rules of Holy Church'.

Princess Anna Comnena is, if possible, even more vitriolic in her accusations against the Bogomils who infested Constantinople around the year 1100. 'The sect of the Bogomils', she writes, 'is very clever in aping virtue.' No 'long‑haired worldlings' were to be found in the sect, because they concealed their cult beneath a monk's cloak and cowl. The Bogomils went about stooping and looking gloomy, and muttering to themselves; but inside they were like ravening wolves. And Anna Comnena adds an interesting note about Basil, the chief of the 'Elect' in Byzantium, who was burnt at the stake by Emperor Alexius Comnenus. He went about, she maintained, with twelve 'apostles', and also a group of female disciples.

Some scholars, notably those with a Marxist background, see elements RATIONALIST of rationalism in Bogomil doctrine and ideology. Thus, Professor D. ELEMENTS Angelov gives a telling essay on the Bogomils the title 'Rationalistic Ideas of a Medieval Heresy'. A good case can be made for this view.

The Bogomils held for example that the rite of baptism, as practised by John the Baptist, had no special virtue, since ordinary water and oil, which possessed no miraculous power, were used. A further reason given by the Bosnian Bogomils for rejecting infant baptism was that babies were incapable of understanding what was going on. A certain rationalistic approach is apparent in the negative attitude to veneration of the Christian Cross: the son, it was argued, should not venerate the object on which his father was killed; again, the Cross was nothing but a piece of common wood, and there was nothing holy about it at all.

About Holy Communion, that central feature of the Christian faith, the Bogomils were quite categorical: its elements were nothing but ordinary bread and wine. The view of the Orthodox Church – that Communion was the great mystery of accepting the body and blood of Christ – was repudiated. The Cathars, the Western dualists who derived from the Bogomils, reacted against Communion even more energetically. They declared that it was comical to think that the body of Christ was received in a mystical manner at Communion. If this occurred, then even a body as large as the biggest mountain on earth would have been eaten up by the faithful long ago.

The Bogomils also rejected the cult of relics. They declared that the bones of dead men differed in no way from the bones of dead animals.

However, these commonsense elements are so inextricably mixed up with medieval superstition and apocryphal legends culled from various sources, that it would be wrong to exaggerate their philosophical value. Where the Bogomils possess the greatest historical importance is in the field of social protest and political action.

SOCIAL ORGANIZA-TION AND POLITICAL ACTION

The Bogomils early learnt that their survival depended on concealment from the hostile State and official Church authorities. They formed themselves into secret societies, of a conspiratorial type, which enhanced the fear and loathing which they inspired in both the Bulgarian and the Byzantine governments. As a result of their intransigent hostility to all feudal or 'capitalist' institutions, the menace of the Bogomils provoked a reaction comparable to that inspired by modern Communist parties among regimes in many parts of the world.

From the very beginning, the Bogomils had a leader known as the *Protos* – 'Notable', or *Protodidaskalos* – 'First Teacher'. The chief

Fig. 24 A medieval Bulgarian shepherd, from the social class from which a substantial part of the Bogomil supporters was drawn. From a fourteenth-century icon in the Rila Monastery. (After Naslednikova)

assistants of the *Protos* were known as Apostles, belonging to the circle of the 'Perfect', and travelling perpetually from place to place to propagate the faith.

The Bogomils formed communities or lodges, rather in the manner of Freemasons. A Western source of the year 1167 speaks of four main fraternities of Bulgarian Bogomils, called Romana, Dragometsia, Meliniqua and Bulgaria. There was also a fraternity in the city of Sredets (Sofia), where the Bogomils and Paulicians staged a revolt in the year 1079, and murdered the bishop, Michael.

Each lodge had its *Dedets*, a sort of bishop. The assistants of the *Dedets* were called *Starets* – 'Elder', or else, *Gost* – 'Visitor'.

The Bogomils constituted themselves the champions of the poor against feudal oppression, and also against the monopoly of wealth and learning exercised by the Orthodox Church. They sought to subvert the royal and Church authorities by preaching against the wealth and pomp of kings and prelates. They contributed towards the undermining of the First Bulgarian Empire in its final phases; under Greek rule, from 1018 to 1185, the movement took on a patriotic hue, and its adepts attacked the agents of Byzantine dominion in Bulgaria. Unfortunately the Bogomils retained their crusading zeal also during the Second Empire, and made a great nuisance of themselves under such rulers as Tsar Boril in the thirteenth century, and Ivan Alexander in the fourteenth. Under the

Muslim Turks, the Bogomils gradually disappeared, largely because their prime enemies, the Bulgarian tsars and the Orthodox Church, had ceased to exist as a dominant power.

It is a matter of dispute how far the Bogomils passed from passive resistance and philosophical anarchism to militant action. In the view of Professor Obolensky, 'there is no reason to believe that they preached anything but a passive resistance to the State. The practice of violence was incompatible not only with their evangelical ideals, but also with dualistic theology . . .' It is true that the Bulgarian Bogomils did not possess a standing army, as did the Paulicians of Asia Minor, or the Albigensians of France. Nevertheless, their political and even military role cannot be altogether ignored. For instance, they made an alliance with the Pechenegs in the year 1086, and apparently encouraged these barbarian invaders to ravage the Balkans. They constituted a 'fifth column' in Bulgaria, both under the Bulgarian tsars, and during Byzantine domination. There is no doubt that they helped to destroy Bulgarian national unity, and pave the way for ultimate Turkish conquest.

THE SPREAD OF BOGOMILISM ABROAD

Immediately to the northwest of Bulgaria, Bogomilism found a fertile soil in the medieval kingdom of Serbia. This was particularly the case during the reign of Zhupan Stephen Nemanya (1168–96), when many villages of serfs were handed over to the control of the monasteries. Resulting dissatisfaction with the feudal order encouraged the introduc‚ tion of Bogomilism, that 'foul and disgusting heresy', as a contemporary source termed it. The Serbs put in hand a special redaction of the Priest Cosmas's discourse against the Bogomils and Archbishop Sava in 1221 convened a Church council at which the doctrines of the 'Babuni' or Serbian Bogomils, were expressly condemned. The Law Code of Tsar Stephen Dushan of Serbia, drawn up in 1349, specifically lays down the punishments to be applied to the Bogomil or Babuni propagandists.

In nearby Bosnia, there was a semi‚official Bogomil Church, with a regular bishop residing at Janici. The Bosnian Bogomils were known as Patarenes, and occasionally, as Kudugeri. The Patarene Church was linked with the national struggle against Hungarian feudal lords, who attempted to subjugate the Bosnians and impose on them the Roman

Catholic faith. Because of their hatred of Catholicism, many of the Bosnian Patarenes preferred to adopt Islam after the Ottoman conquest.

In Kievan Russia, Cosmas's discourse against the Bogomils was widely circulated. It was found effective by the Russian Orthodox clergy in combatting other types of heresy and pagan survivals, which lingered on after the conversion of Russia under St Vladimir in 989.

The principal offshoots of the Bogomils of Bulgaria were the heretical sects known as the Albigensians in southern France and the Cathars in Germany and northern Italy. The links between the Bulgarians, and the Cathars and Albigensians, were already known to the Roman Catholic Inquisition of those days. An Italian ex-heretic, Rainier Sacchoni, who wrote about the year 1230, tells of an Italian 'bishop' called Nazarius, who was educated in Bulgaria, and held that the Virgin Mary was an angel. This Nazarius brought back from Bulgaria to his community at Concorezzo the Bogomil heretical book, *The Gospel of John*.

It was proved by the Bulgarian scholar Yordan Ivanov that the Cathar apocryphal treatise, *The Vision of Isaiah*, was a direct translation from a Bulgarian Slavonic original. Sacchoni goes so far as to declare roundly that all the heretic churches of the West in his time have their origin in Bulgaria and Dugunthia, by which he meant Dragovitsa and Tragurium. Byzantium also played a role, as we see from reports of a Cathar council which took place in 1167 near Toulouse: a certain Nikita from Constantinople attended as the chairman of the council, and promoted and consecrated a number of 'Believers' into the ranks of the 'Perfect'.

CHAPTER VI

Literature and Learning

We have already drawn attention to the heritage of the Bulgarian lands in monuments of Classical Greek, Latin and Christian Byzantine epigraphy, philosophy and culture generally. Reference has also been made to important texts inscribed on stone by the pagan Bulgar khans in Greek, incorporating a number of Turco-Bulgar terms and expressions.

None of this material sufficed to fulfil the long-term spiritual aspira-tions and educational demands posed by the creation of the united Slavo-Bulgar state by Khan Asparukh late in the seventh century, and its final adoption of Christianity on the Byzantine model under Khan Boris-Michael in the year 864 (or 865).

MISSIONS OF CYRIL AND METHODIUS

That Bulgaria eventually became the main repository of the Christian Slavonic legacy of St Cyril and St Methodius, was the result of a long series of historical circumstances, some of them fortuitous. It is in fact rather misleading to include an essay on 'Creation of the Slav Script' in a symposium entitled *Bulgaria's share in human culture*, as was done by Professor Emil Georgiev. The brothers Cyril and Methodius were from Salonica; and although their inborn feeling for Slavonic culture and their mastery of various Slavonic and other langugages and dialects was truly remarkable, they cannot be classed as Bulgarians, though they evidently had Slavonic blood in their veins.

Born in 827, Constantine was marked out for a brilliant career. As a young man, he was appointed librarian of the Church of Saint Sophia in Constantinople. While still in his twenties, he succeeded the patriarch Photius as professor of philosophy at the University of Constantinople – hence his appellation 'the Philosopher'. Constantine's exceptional talents both as a linguist and a negotiator were recognized by his appoint-ment as special envoy to the Arabs in the year 855, and then to the Khazars in southern Russia, in the course of which he visited Cherson on the Black Sea, and recovered the alleged relics of St Clement. Accompanied by his brother Methodius, Constantine successfully reached the Khazar khagan's court, and held disputes with Jewish and

Muslim religious leaders on the question of the true faith. All this gave Constantine useful insight into the Arabic and Hebrew languages; we gather that he also had some slight knowledge of Armenian, Georgian and possibly Coptic.

This mission to the Khazars was a sign of the increased importance of Russian and Slavonic affairs. In 860, the Russians staged a dangerous naval assault on Constantinople. At the same time, the Bulgarians under Khan Boris were beginning to take an interest in Christianity, though they had a worrying habit of cultivating friendly relations with the Pope in Rome, rather than dealing solely with Orthodox Byzantium.

At this juncture, in 862, an unexpected embassy arrived in Constantinople from Prince Rastislav of Moravia, a territory comprising a central region of Czechoslovakia. Rastislav had decided to free his land from alien German and Frankish ecclesiastical and political propaganda, which was directed to paving the way for the dominance of German feudal lords. Wishing also to give his local Church a Slavonic character, by establishing a Slav clergy and a Slav liturgy set down in Slavonic letters, he asked Emperor Michael III to send missionaries to teach his people the sacred literature in their own Slavonic tongue.

Emperor Michael immediately perceived the political and ecclesiastical potentialities of the situation. He sent for Constantine and Methodius and urged them to go to Moravia as his envoys, adding: 'You are both natives of Thessalonica, and all Thessalonians speak pure Slav.' The brothers accepted the mission, and Constantine (who by now had assumed the name of Cyril) set rapidly to work on completing a Slavonic version of the Liturgical Gospel, which is a selection of lessons from the Four Gospels, intended for use in church services.

The idiom used by Cyril for his translation was forged from the spoken tongue of the Macedonian Slavs, which was then far more intelligible to the Slavs of Central Europe than it would be today. However, much of the literary syntax and philosophical terminology had to be created specially by reference to Byzantine Greek, so that Cyril must be credited not only with devising the Slavonic alphabet, and Old Church Slavonic literature, but with the entire creation of written Slavonic as a viable, evolving medium of literary communication. By the perpetuation of the national idiom in written form the Slavs were saved from the threat of assimilation by more powerful or more advanced

Fig. 25

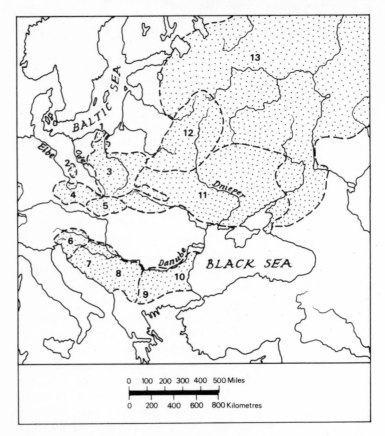

Fig. 25 *Distribution of spoken Slavonic languages in Europe, 1 Kashubian; 2 Lusa-tian; 3 Polish; 4 Czech; 5 Slovakian; 6 Slovenian; 7 Croatian; 8 Serbian; 9 Macedonian; 10 Bulgarian; 11 Ukrainian; 12 Byelorussian; 13 Russian. (After Gimbutas)*

neighbours. This fact explains the extraordinary veneration accorded to the canonized Cyril and Methodius not only by the Slavs of Macedonia and Central Europe, but by those of Bulgaria, Poland, Russia and all other members of the Slavonic community of peoples.

Two ancient Slavonic alphabets, the Cyrillic and the Glagolitic, date from the time of Cyril or shortly afterwards. The Cyrillic derives from the Greek uncial or capital letters, with the addition of letters to express sounds in the Slavonic tongues not contained in Greek. It has proved the more vigorous of the two, and is still used, with minor

Fig. 26

modifications, in the Soviet Union, Bulgaria and Serbia today. Glagolitic, on the other hand, is a much more artificial creation, based on a rounded, curly type of Greek minuscule writing, though having the same sound values as are conveyed by the Cyrillic alphabet. It developed mostly among the West and Southwest Slav communities, and did not continue in current use beyond the seventeenth century.

Many scholars now reject the traditional view that Cyril devised Cyrillic, and favour the idea that his alphabet was the Glagolitic, while Cyrillic was evolved later, perhaps by St Clement of Ohrida. In general, history teaches us that uncial, monumental alphabets habitually emerge first, for the purpose of inscribing on stone, bark or other primitive materials, while cursive alphabets, for connected writing on paper or parchment, generally come later. Cyrillic clearly derives from Greek uncials, and might be taken for an earlier invention than Glagolitic, which was partly adapted from Greek cursive script. A point of interest is that the gradual substitution of the Greek minuscule for uncial writing – a reform which for its cultural significance has been compared to the later invention of printing – took place in Byzantium in the reign of Emperor Theophilus, who ruled from 829 to 842, while Cyril was still a boy.

One possible explanation is that Cyril first evolved Cyrillic, from Greek uncials, while still working on Byzantine territory and preparatory to proceeding to Moravia. On arrival there, he encountered strong opposition among the Frankish clergy, who branded his writings in their Cyrillic guise as unacceptable and heretical. Cyril and Methodius, if we accept this version, would have been obliged hurriedly to evolve a new alphabet – the Glagolitic – which outwardly hardly resembles Greek at all, and is also far more difficult to decipher than Cyrillic; it thus acquires the character of a cryptogram or secret writing, unintelligible to the uninitiated. Many of the original Greek letters, in fact, appear in Glagolitic in reversed form, a characteristic of secret writing. A vague uniformity was imparted to the Glagolitic by lavish use of loops. Sir Steven Runciman goes so far as to remark, rather aptly, that the only merit of Glagolitic is that it suited a particular political crisis!

In Moravia, and later in Venice and Rome, Cyril and Methodius had occasion to do battle with fundamentalist propounders of what is called the 'three languages heresy' – namely, the idea that it is permissible

Cyrillic	Numerical value	Glagolitic (rounded)	Glagolitic (angular)	Numerical value	Slavonic name of letter	Transcription
ⰀА	1	ⰀⰀ	ⰀⰀ	1	азъ	a
Б	—	Б	Б	2	боукы	b
в	2	Ⰲ	Ш	3	вѣдѣ	v
г	3	Ⰳ	Ⰳ	4	глаголи	g
д	4	Ⰴ	Ⰴ	5	добро	d
е	5	Э	Э	6	юстъ	e
ж	—	Ⰶ	Ⰶ	7	живѣте	ž
ѕ	6	Ⰷ	Ⰷ	8	sѣло	ʒ
з	7	Ⰸ	Ⰸ	9	земла	z
и	8	Ⰹ	Ⰹ	20	иже	i
і	10	Ⰻ	Ⰻ			i
ⱖ	—	Ⰺ	Ⰺ	10	і	i
ħ	—	Ⰼ	ПР	30	děrvъ	ǵ
к	20	Ⰽ	Ⰽ	40	како	k
л	30	Ⰾ	Ⰾ	50	людиѥ	l
м	40	Ⰿ	Ⰿ	60	мыслите	m

Cyrillic	Numerical value	Glagolitic (rounded)	Glagolitic (angular)
н	50	Ⱀ	Ⱀ
о	70	Ⱁ	Ⱁ
п	80	Ⱂ	Ⱂ
ҁ	90	—	—
р	100	ь	Ⱃ
с	200	Ⱄ	Ⱄ
т	300	Ⱅ	Ⱅ
оу	400	Ⱆ	Ⱆ
ȣ	400	—	—
ф	500	ф	ф
х	600	ь	Ⱈ
ѡ	800	Ⱉ	Ⱉ
ψ	—	Ⱋ	Ⱋ
ц	900	Ⱌ	Ⱌ
ч	90	Ⱍ	Ⱍ
ш	—	Ⱎ	Ⱎ
ъ	—	Ⱐ	Ⱐ

Fig. 26 The Cyrillic and Glagolitic alphabets, based on a table published by the Czechoslovak Academy of Sciences, Prague

Numerical value	Slavonic name of letter	Transcription
70	нашь	n
80	онъ	o
90	покои	p
—	—	—
100	рьци	r
200	слово	s
300	тврьдо	t
400	оукъ	u
—		u
500	фрьтъ	f
600	хѣръ	ch
700	штъ	o
800	ща	št
900	ци	c
1000	чрьвь	č
—	ша	š
—	юр'ъ	ъ

Cyrillic	Numerical value	Glagolitic (rounded)	Glagolitic (angular)	Numerical value	Slavonic name of letter	Transcription
Ъι	—	ꙗⱇ	—	—	юрьι	y
Ъι	—	ꙗⱎ	—	—		y
ЪИ	—	ꙗⱖ	—	—		y
ь	—	Ⱐ	Ⰹ		юрь	ь
ѣ	—	Ⰴ	Ⰺ	—	ıать	ě
ю	—	Ⱂ	Ⱎ	—		ju
ıа	—	—	—	—		ja
ıє	—	—	—	—		je
Ѧ	900	Ⰵ	—	—		ę
Ѫ	—	Ⱑ	—	—		ę
Ж	—	Ⱔ	—	—		ǫ
ıѧ	—	Ⰵ	Ⰵ	—		ję
ıѫ	—	Ⱔ	—	—		jǫ
а̃	60	—	—	—	а̃и	x
ѱ	700	—	—	—	ѱи	ps
Ѳ	9	Ⱚ	Ⱚ	—	ѳита	f
ѵ	400	ⰲ	—	—	ижица	υ

to celebrate the divine office only in Hebrew, Greek and Latin, since these are the three tongues in which the inscription was written by Pontius Pilate on Christ's Cross. This ridiculous notion was countered by Cyril and Methodius with a wealth of reasoning and rhetoric, supported by quotations from Chapter XIV of St Paul's First Epistle to the Corinthians:

> . . . For if I pray in an unknown tongue, my spirit prayeth, but my understanding is unfruitful . . . Yet in the church I had rather speak five words with my understanding, that by my voice I might teach others also, than ten thousand words in an unknown tongue.

This championing of the rights of the Slavonic tongue as a medium of culture and worship was of especial relevance in Bulgaria, which was to undergo centuries of Turkish political dominance, and Phanariot Greek hegemony in the ecclesiastical field.

It is worth remarking that Cyril and Methodius are still venerated in Rome, where Cyril died in 869 at the early age of forty-two. They had brought with them from the Crimea the relics of St Clement, pope and martyr, which were re-interred in Rome with great pomp. Ancient frescoes and a mosaic depicting Cyril and Methodius still survive there, and they were both canonized by the Roman Catholic Church.

On his deathbed, Cyril implored Methodius to resist the temptation to return to Byzantium and urged him to continue their common work for the Slavs. Pope Hadrian II appointed Methodius archbishop of Pannonia and papal legate to the Slavonic nations. However, the last fifteen years of Methodius's life and ministry were embittered by the merciless onslaught of foes both political and ecclesiastical. In 870 Rastislav's nephew Svatopluk overthrew and blinded his uncle, the patron and protector of Cyril and Methodius. On his return to Moravia from Rome, Methodius was imprisoned for three years at the instigation of the Frankish and Bavarian clergy, and only freed as a result of papal intervention. However, even the papacy became lukewarm towards the cause of the Slavonic vernacular liturgy, especially after the death of John VIII (872–82). In 881, Methodius made a journey to consult with Emperor Basil I in Constantinople; back in Moravia, he died exhausted and discouraged four years later.

The last few years of Methodius's life were occupied with translating a large body of biblical and liturgical work into Slavonic from the Greek. This was to become an integral part of Old Bulgarian literature. Methodius was assisted by his disciples, Gorazd (a Moravian Slav, whom he had appointed as his successor), Laurence, Clement (later St Clement of Ohrida), Nahum, and Angelarius. Methodius had already helped Cyril to render into Slavonic the Greek liturgical offices and the New Testament. During this last period of his life and work, Methodius translated the canonical books of the Old Testament, selected writings from the Greek Fathers, and the *Nomocanon*, a Byzantine manual of canon law and imperial edicts on Church matters.

To this rich legacy, all of which was later taken over and cherished by the Bulgarians, must be added the translations and original writings which Cyril himself had managed to complete before his premature death. Prominent among these is his beautiful complete rendering of the Four Gospels – the first translation of the Gospels into a vernacular language to appear in the West. This is introduced by a special poetic introduction, called the *Proglas*. Its text was discovered in 1858 in a Serbian parchment manuscript from the fourteenth century, where the composition is ascribed to Constantine the Philosopher – Cyril's regular title as a layman. Though some scholars attributed it to the early Bulgarian writer Constantine of Preslav, Father Francis Dvornik and other reliable authorities favour the attribution to Cyril. This *Proglas* has a special rhythmic quality, and reflects the underlying ideas that inspired Cyril in his life-work: above all, a passionate appeal to the Slavs to cherish books written in their own language. Also composed by Cyril were the discourse on the recovery of the relics of St Clement from Cherson on the Black Sea, and a 'Tract on the True Faith', which he used in his missionary endeavours. Several other writings by Cyril are listed in his *Vita*, but ostensibly disappeared during the pogrom against Slavonic letters and culture which took place there following the death of Methodius in 885.

The death of Methodius was the signal for a concerted onslaught on the Slav missionaries by the jealous Frankish and German clerics, abetted by the Moravian Prince Svatopluk. Beaten up and imprisoned, some of the disciples of Methodius were then sold into slavery and taken to Venice; others – notably Clement, Nahum and Angelarius –

eventually made their way down the Danube on a raft, and arrived at Pliska via Belgrade, then a Bulgarian outpost.

Plates 6–8,
Fig. 29

The arrival of these experienced missionaries in Pliska was a great event in the history of Slavonic culture in Bulgaria. The young Bulgarian Church was still predominantly Greek in character and in personnel, and lacked any sustained Slavonic liturgical tradition. The nationalist element headed by the old pagan Turco-Bulgar nobility was still strong. The implanting of the Cyrillo-Methodian tradition thus provided stimulus for a new upsurge of Christian worship, in the Slavonic vernacular familiar to the majority of the population.

Angelarius having died soon afterwards of his sufferings and priva- tions, it was decided that Clement should spread the good word in southern Macedonia, in the Ohrida region, while Nahum remained behind for the time being at Pliska, the Bulgar capital. During his thirty years' ministry in Macedonia, Clement is said to have trained some 3,500 pupils, so it is only natural that the present-day University of Sofia should bear his name. On the accession of Tsar Symeon in 893, Clement was made a bishop – the first Slavonic bishop in Bulgaria. Nahum was sent to assist Clement, which he did most devotedly until his death in 906. The monastery of the Holy Archangels on Lake Ohrida, where he is buried, was built by Nahum and is a memorial to his zeal. Clement died in 916, aged about eighty.

LITERARY
WORK OF
ST CLEMENT
OF OHRIDA

Clement's literary productivity was truly prodigious, if one takes into account his teaching programme, his missionary journeys in the Mace- donian provinces, his building of churches, and enormous administra- tive responsibilities. From the Greek he translated those parts of the Scriptures and the Byzantine liturgy which Cyril and Methodius had not managed to render into Slavonic. Clement's own sermons and homilies for special occasions are the foundations of original Bulgarian literature. His eulogies are fine examples of rhetorical style, and are rendered all the more effective by a number of ingenious devices, such as that of apostrophizing a pair of saints alternately, producing an anti- phonal effect. Sometimes Clement will pull out all the organ-stops of majestic power, and his repetition of sonorous basic words – as in the phrase 'he thundered like thunder' – produce effects calculated to put the fear of God into the simple peasants of Macedonia. At other times, he will emphasize the gentle, mellifluous side of Christian preaching, as when he utters the eulogy of St Cyril, declaring 'I envy thy many-voiced tongue, through which flowed spiritual sweetness for all peoples . . .' Clement also wrote a eulogy of St Demetrius of Salonica, who is supposed to have saved the native city of Cyril and Methodius from attack by heathen Slav and Bulgar hordes.

Clement of Ohrida, to whom we owe extended biographies of his teachers, Cyril and Methodius, employed the Glagolitic script for his writings, though they were soon transcribed into Cyrillic, which in 893 was adopted as the official Bulgarian alphabet under Tsar Symeon. So authoritative and so popular did Clement's eulogies of saints become, that many of them were wrongly attributed by the scribes to St John Chrysostom. Clement's fame spread all over the Slavonic world, and especially into Russia after its adoption of the Christian faith in 989; many of the oldest and best copies of Clement's works are found in ancient Russian manuscripts. The Bulgarian Academy of Sciences has embarked on a critical edition of St Clement's writings, edited by Professors B. St. Angelov, K. M. Kuev, and Khr. Kodov, the first volume of which appeared in Sofia in 1970.

While Clement was enriching Old Bulgarian literature in Ohrida, a flourishing school of writers grew up at Tsar Symeon's capital of Preslav, in northeastern Bulgaria. The Cyrillic alphabet was here officially in use, and there are minor differences in grammar and style which distinguish the Preslav from the Ohrida tradition. THE GOLDEN AGE OF BULGARIAN LITERATURE

One eminent writer was Constantine, bishop of Preslav. This Constantine seems to have known Methodius, so was probably born around the middle of the ninth century; he was also a friend of Nahum of Ohrida.

Constantine of Preslav's best known work is called the Didactic Gospel. Composed about 894, the work is partly original, partly a compilation. It contains the so-called 'Alphabet Prayer', also a foreword and an introduction, a series of *besedi* (talks on Gospel subjects), the *Tserkovno skazanie* or 'Ecclesiastical Legend' and then a chronology of world history from Adam and Eve down to the year it was written. The *besedi* are designed for use in church services on specific Sundays of the Orthodox calendar; thirty-eight have been identified as adaptations of sermons by St Cyril of Alexandria; one only is thought to have been composed independently by Constantine of Preslav himself.

Bishop Constantine of Preslav was a vigorous controversialist. He translated from Greek into Old Bulgarian a tract entitled *Four sermons against the Arians*. This work marks the beginning of a polemical tradition in Old Bulgarian literature, a tradition that was to gain in importance as time went on, under the impact of the Bogomil heresy. Constantine also translated a Byzantine manual of church organization, and composed a special commemoration service in memory of St Methodius.

Much credit for the achievements of the Preslav school belongs to Tsar Symeon himself. The Old Russian selection of the Church Fathers' writings called the *Compilation of Svyatoslav*, made in Kiev in 1073, states that this anthology was originally put together at Symeon's express command. In some quarters he is even credited with having written a brief but telling defence of Slavonic letters under the pseudonym of Chernorizets Khrabăr, which means literally 'the Monk named Brave (or Bold)'. There has been much speculation about the true identity of the author, whose fame rests on a single work scarcely four pages long – the Discourse *O Pismenakh* ('On Letters'). Composed at the turn of the ninth century, it states that people who knew Cyril and Methodius were still alive. With self-confidence and panache, Khrabăr leaps to the defence of the Slavonic alphabet and Church literature, against the bigots who still dared to adhere to the 'three languages heresy'. Probably these opponents were representatives of the Byzantine Greek clergy active in Bulgaria, who opposed the introduction of liturgy in the Slavonic vernacular.

Khrabăr has earned undying renown among the Bulgarians by his ingenious reasoning, according to which the Slavonic letters are not only equal in excellence to the Greek alphabet, but even superior to it. The Greek alphabet, he states, was created in several stages by pagan Hellenes; the Slavonic, by contrast, was invented in a short time by one man, Constantine the Philosopher, a great Christian saint. The robust tone and exuberant self-confidence of Khrabăr's concise discourse command attention, as the manifesto of a young nation on the brink of cultural maturity.

A third outstanding figure of the Preslav school was Ioan Ekzarkh Bălgarski, or John the Exarch, who was born around the middle of the ninth century, and died about the year 925. Virtually nothing is known about this important writer and translator's personal life. Even his official title of 'Exarch' has given rise to difficulty, since it could mean either that John was a high official, a kind of Apostolic Delegate to Bulgaria, or else the abbot of a leading monastery.

In 891–92, John the Exarch translated into Old Bulgarian the treatise *On the Orthodox Faith*, by St John of Damascus. He added an interesting preface of his own. The Slavonic version is usually known as *Nebesa* ('The Heavens'), and provided useful information about natural phenomena, as well as about the Orthodox faith itself.

No less valuable was John the Exarch's account of the six days of the Creation, called the *Shestodnev*, or Hexameron. Although based partly on St John Chrysostom and St Basil the Great, this treatise has much original material on geography, human anatomy, and the marvels of human existence.

John the Exarch was an enthusiastic supporter of Tsar Symeon's plans for developing Preslav as a great Christian city. He devotes much of the preface of the sixth oration of the *Shestodnev* to this theme. He was also the author of a number of *Slova* (homilies and sermons), which have been appearing since 1971 in an annotated edition.

The destruction of Great Preslav, first by the Russians and then by the Byzantines in the second half of the tenth century, and the downfall of the First Bulgarian Empire early in the eleventh, did not put a stop to this wonderful flowering of patristic and liturgical literature. The role of Ohrida as a centre of Slavonic letters continued even under the Byzantines. A large number of ancient manuscripts in Church Slavonic, dating from the eleventh and twelfth centuries have been attributed to Macedonian scriptoria, while others were copied out in secret places in East Bulgaria and elsewhere.

Among the most famous Old Bulgarian manuscripts of this period are the Glagolitic *Codex Assemanianus* containing the Evangelarium or liturgical Gospel readings; the *Psalterium Sinaiticum*, containing the Psalms, and the *Euchologion Sinaiticum*, comprising the Euchologium; further, the well-known *Rila Fragments*.

Among Cyrillic manuscripts of this early period, pride of place belongs to such monuments as the *Codex Suprasliensis*, the largest extant

SOME
FAMOUS
MANU-
SCRIPTS

Fig. 27

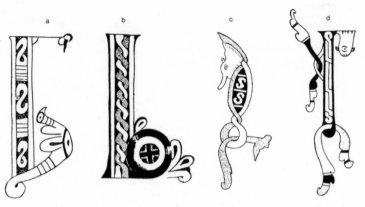

Fig. 27 Decorated capital letters from early Bulgarian (Church Slavonic) manuscripts in Cyrillic (a) and Glagolitic (b, c, d) characters. (After Mirchev and Kodov)

manuscript volume in Old Bulgarian literature; and the *Savvina Kniga* or Savva Gospel Book. There is also the *Codex Eninensis*; this was discovered in 1960 in an ancient church at the village of Enina, near Kazanluk; much damaged, it contains the so-called *Praxapostolus*, an anthology of passages from the epistles of St Paul.

APOCRYPHAL   Alongside canonical literature of the Bulgarian Church there was a
AND WISDOM   wealth of apocryphal works of all kinds, of Eastern wisdom literature,
LITERATURE   and of historical chronicles, mostly of Byzantine Greek origin.

The apocryphal works are associated with both Old Testament and New Testament themes. To the former category belong the Book of Enoch, the Apocalypse of Baruch and the Book of the Twelve Patriarchs. New Testament apocrypha include the Gospels of Nicodemus and Thomas, the latter purporting to describe the childhood of Christ. 'The Virgin's visit to Hell' gives an account of the Virgin Mary's tour of the infernal regions, where she sees the terrible punishment meted out to sinners. She begs Christ to have mercy on the damned, and He grants them relief each year, from Maundy Thursday until Whit Sunday. Again, we have the 'Tale of the Wood of the Cross', which traces the timber of Christ's Cross and that of the two thieves back to the three trunks of a single tree which stood in the Garden of Eden.

It was through Old Bulgarian that the Slavonic world became acquainted with many international works of fable and wisdom. From Byzantium, the Bulgarians took the story of Alexis, Man of God. Alexis is a young man who abandons his possessions and all his family, including his young bride, and departs to live in poverty in a foreign land. For the sake of his religion, he endures all manner of misery. Many years later, Alexis returns home in his old age, but his family fails to recognize him until he is on his death-bed.

A similar theme of renunciation underlies the Story of Varlaam and Ioasaf, or Barlaam and Josaphat. This Indian tale, which reached Byzantium through the medium of Georgian, tells the story of the young Buddha and his Great Renunciation. The whole work has taken on a Christian hue, and preaches the virtues of asceticism and self-denial, stressing the transitory nature of the world in which we live.

A notorious heretical work, now extant only in Latin translation, is the Bogomil catechism known as the *Gospel of John*, or *The Secret Book*, to which reference has already been made. Cast in the form of answers given by Jesus Christ to John 'your brother' at the Last Supper, this work expounds with a certain biblical power the Bogomil notions on the ancestry of Satan, on the Creation, and on the Second Coming of Christ and the Last Judgement. As noted in the previous chapter, the Bogomils and their teaching gave rise to an important Old Bulgarian polemical literature, composed by Orthodox clerics to discredit the heresy. Most noteworthy is the discourse against the Bogomils, by Cosmas the Priest. Many years later we have the *Sinodik*, or proceedings of Tsar Boril's ecclesiastical council of 1211, invoking anathema against the Bogomils and their errors.

As time went on, the Bulgarians became acquainted with such books as the Tale of Ahikar the Wise, which has its roots in ancient Assyria and Babylon. They also composed the lives of their own local saints, in particular St John of Rila (*c.* 876–946), who began life as a simple shepherd, before attaining sanctity in the hills surrounding what is now Bulgaria's most famous monastery.

Fig. 24
Plates 25–27

History and legend were frequently mingled in the popular mind. A favourite work was the romance of Alexander the Great, composed originally by pseudo-Callisthenes, and popular in Bulgaria in its

HISTORY
AND
SCIENCE

Slavonic version. Comparable to this work were stories connected with the siege of Troy.

Old Bulgarian translations of Byzantine Greek chronicles were made, including those of the ninth-century scholar George Hamartolus and George Syncellus who died about the year 810.

Of considerable historical interest is the story known as 'the Miracle of the Bulgarian'. Written in the tenth century, the story concerns a private soldier in the army of Tsar Symeon of Bulgaria and his adventures in a war against the Hungarians. A vision leads the soldier to find three hoops under his dead horse's knee, and from these he fashions a cross endowed with miraculous power.

The spread of literacy brought with it enhanced interest in science and natural history, albeit on a rather unsophisticated level. A fruit of this interest is the Old Slavonic version of the medieval *Physiologus* or 'Bestiary', which is an account of scores of varieties of beasts, birds, reptiles and fishes, with the addition (in some recensions) of a section on stones and minerals. Regarded as natural history, the Bestiary is rather naive, and the descriptions of even common domestic animals show little power of observation. But there is a wealth of imaginative fantasy, as in the depiction of the sirens and dragons, the mantichora or man-headed lion, and the caladrius, a bird which on being brought to a sick man's bedside will foretell his recovery or impending death by turning its head towards or away from the invalid. It is in the *Physiologus* that we can trace the origins of such concepts as that of 'crocodile tears', which this reptile is supposed to shed when it devours a man; or of the mother bear licking her formless cubs into shape.

Another popular pseudo-scientific work was the *Razumnik* or 'Clever Man', variously but wrongly attributed to John Chrysostom, Gregory of Nazianzus and Basil the Great. This discusses, among other things, the composition and size of the sun, the moon and the stars, the distance between heaven and earth, divination by means of natural phenomena, and the creation of Adam and Eve.

THE SILVER AGE OF BULGARIAN LITERATURE The re-establishment of Bulgarian independence under the Assen family towards the end of the twelfth century after nearly two centuries of Byzantine domination, with consequent discouragement of Slavonic vernacular literature, heralded a revival in Bulgarian literary activity.

Under Tsar Ivan Assen II (1218–41), some magnificent Slavonic manuscripts were copied and illuminated. Approximately to this period, for instance, belongs the Bologna Psalter, recently published by the Bulgarian Academy of Sciences (see bibliography under Duichev).

What may be termed the Silver Age of Bulgarian literature and culture was inaugurated by Tsar Ivan Alexander (1331–71). A great patron of the arts, Ivan Alexander commissioned a number of illuminated manuscripts, including the splendid Gospel Book now in the British Museum, and the codex of the Slavonic version of the Chronicle or 'Historical Synopsis' of Constantine Manasses, preserved in the Vatican library.

Plates 48, 50

The last flowering of medieval Bulgarian literature is associated also with the name of Patriarch Euthymius, the leader of the Bulgarian people in adversity. Euthymius is one of the heroic figures of the period, but strangely enough this vigorous and patriotic character allied himself with a thoroughly decadent and degenerate movement in the Byzantine Church, namely that of 'Hesychasm'. This term is derived from the Greek word *hesychia* ('quietude'), used by Eastern Christian mystics to describe the state of recollection and inner silence which follows man's victory over his passions and leads him, through contemplative prayer, to the knowledge of God. In practice, the Hesychasts came to resemble the Indian fakirs or holy men, who sit aimlessly around on their spiky mats, contemplating their navels. In fact, the Hesychasts themselves were nicknamed *umbilis animi*, or people with their souls in their navels.

EUTHYMIUS
AND THE
HESYCHAST
MOVEMENT

The connexion of Bulgaria with the Hesychast movement began about 1330, when St Gregory of Sinai, a leading Byzantine Hesychast ascetic, founded a community in the remote region of Paroria, in the Strandzha Mountains of southeastern Bulgaria. One of Gregory's disciples was the Bulgarian, St Theodosius of Tărnovo, who learnt the technique of asceticism and mystical prayer under the master, at Paroria. After Gregory's death, Theodosius settled at Kilifarevo, not far from Great Tărnovo. With the help of Tsar Ivan Alexander, he founded a seat of learning there, the renown of which spread to Serbia, Hungary and Romania, and to the Black Sea ports, such as Nessebăr.

One of the disciples of Theodosius was Euthymius, who became Bulgaria's last medieval patriarch. In 1363, Euthymius accompanied

Theodosius to Constantinople, and then spent some time on Mount Athos imbibing the Hesychast doctrine at its source. In 1371, he was disgraced and arrested by order of the Byzantine emperor. Expelled from Byzantium, Euthymius returned to Great Tărnovo and founded the Holy Trinity monastery, where he set up a notable literary school. He was elected patriarch of Bulgaria in 1375.

Euthymius won general acclaim as the leader of Bulgarian intellectual life, both as a teacher, as a reviser of the Slavonic liturgical texts and as an original writer, notably in the field of hagiography. He favoured an ornate style, and tried to make Slavonic sacred texts conform more closely to their Greek originals, while also admiring the pure style of Cyril and Methodius, whose memory he venerated. Euthymius recorded the lives

Plate 27

of several of his country's saints, that of St John of Rila being prefaced by a treatise on the ascetic life. He also wrote a noteworthy panegyric of Constantine the Great and St Helena. Following the Ottoman siege of Tărnovo, in the defence of which Euthymius himself took part, the

Plate 28

great patriarch was deposed and exiled to the Bachkovo monastery in southern Bulgaria where he died in 1402.

DISCIPLES
OF
PATRIARCH
EUTHYMIUS

The work of Patriarch Euthymius was continued by a number of disciples, notable among whom was the Bulgarian monk Cyprian Tsamblak. In 1375, Cyprian was appointed archbishop of Kiev, then, from 1390 to 1406, he was Metropolitan of Moscow and All Russia. As head of the Russian Church, he encouraged the acquisition of South Slavonic manuscripts by Russian monastery libraries, thus saving many important Old Bulgarian texts from destruction by the Turks. He imitated the literary style and techniques of Euthymius, and reformed Russian orthography. Cyprian initiated the compilation of the first comprehensive Muscovite chronicle, and drew up a list of forbidden heretical books.

A nephew of Cyprian, Gregory Tsamblak, was likewise a disciple of Euthymius, and his eulogies of saints are held in high esteem. At one time Gregory was abbot of Dechani in Serbia, where he wrote a biography of the martyred Serbian king Stephen Urosh III. He later worked in Moldavia, moving in 1406 to Lithuania. Here he supported the local ruler, who wished to set up a separate Orthodox Church in his realm. Against the express command of the Constantinople patriarchate, which even went to the length of excommunicating him, the Lithuanian bishops elected Gregory Metropolitan of Kiev, a post which he held from 1415 until his death in 1420.

Yet another follower of Euthymius was Ioasaph of Vidin (or Ioasaf Bdinski), appointed Metropolitan of that city in 1392. He composed a eulogy of St Philothea, basing it largely on Euthymius's own life of that saint. This work was written in 1395, to commemorate the transfer of St Philothea's remains from Tărnovo to Vidin, and Ioasaph includes a lament over the capture of Tărnovo by the Turks in 1393.

Finally, mention should be made of that eccentric figure Constantine of Kostenets, who was educated at Bachkovo monastery by one of the pupils of Euthymius. Around 1410, the Turks forced him to flee to Serbia, where he was kindly received by King Stefan Lazarevich (reigned 1389–1427), whose biography Constantine later wrote. Apart from his account of a journey to Palestine, Constantine is best known for his treatise on Slavonic languages and literatures, *On Letters* (1418). Professor Dimitri Obolensky describes this work, with barbed accuracy, as 'the work of a poor historian and of a linguistic pedant'. Constantine believed that the language of Cyril and Methodius was basically Russian, with an admixture of six other Slav tongues; and that sacred languages form a family, in which Hebrew, Greek and the Slavonic ones are the father, the mother and the offspring respectively. He further insisted that Slavonic writing should ape Greek models with the utmost literalness. There is little serious value in Constantine's theories, but they make quite amusing reading. He invents fanciful explanations of individual Slavonic letters, and likens diacritical marks to ladies' hats!

The Turkish conquest of Bulgaria at the end of the fourteenth century destroyed the environment and conditions necessary for the further evolution of a national literature. Nevertheless, Bulgarian culture continued to survive not only in Macedonia and Serbia, but also in Russia. In Romania, a specifically Bulgar‑Wallachian literature flourished from the fifteenth to the seventeenth century, so that most of the genres of Old Bulgarian continued to develop north of the Danube.

CHAPTER VII

Architecture and the Arts

Bulgaria offers material of exceptional interest to the student of art and architecture. Excavations over the last century have turned up examples of art and material culture dating from all major periods of human history, from the Old Stone Age onwards. The cultural history of the Classical world can scarcely be studied without reference to Bulgaria's Thracian, Hellenistic and Roman remains, which provide valuable evidence on sculpture, metalwork, painting, architecture and town planning in ancient times.

Plates 1–3

This book is devoted almost exclusively to the period of Bulgarian cultural history stretching from the arrival of Asparukh and the proto-Bulgars in the seventh century AD, up to the Turkish conquest at the close of the fourteenth. We shall, however, treat briefly of later monu-ments where these represent a continuation of ancient Bulgarian artistic traditions.

It might be thought a simple task to identify the main monuments of Bulgarian culture, and assign them to their correct periods. Unfortunately this is not always the case. To take one notorious example, a small coterie has for years maintained, against all the probabilities, that the metro-politan palace of Aboba-Pliska is not a Bulgar, but a Romano-Byzantine creation, and that the Madara Horseman, that unique expression of proto-Bulgar national pride, is really a Thracian monu-ment! Much energy has had to be wasted on the refutation of such fantasies.

ARCHITEC-
TURE OF THE
PLISKA-
MADARA
PERIOD

The might of the pagan khans of the Bulgars was centred on north-eastern Bulgaria, the modern Shumen district, in the hinterland of Varna. Their headquarters was sited at Pliska, which is on an undulating plain, the city and outer stockade having once covered an area of nine square miles.

Pliska had earlier contained a Byzantine settlement, abandoned in face of the marauding Slavs who overran the area in the sixth century.

The Slavs themselves built little more than simple huts, with mud and wattle walls, and a thatched roof, though they were also capable of erecting wooden barns.

It was left to the proto-Bulgar Khan Asparukh (679–701) with his sense of regal destiny, to set up a metropolis which would proclaim the glory of the new State. In so doing, Asparukh also had in mind to perpetuate architectural and ceremonial traditions of the Sasanian monarchs of Iran, with whom the ancient Bulgars had had many links, before the Sasanians were overthrown by the Arab caliphs in AD 642. The Bulgars' ultimate ambition was to create a metropolis rivalling Constantinople itself, though the geographical situation is very different. Perhaps a more pertinent comparison would be with the 'Umayyad palaces and citadels of Syria, which are contemporary with Pliska, and are also distinguished by the use of massive ashlar masonry blocks, and by skilful mastery of drainage and hot water systems, complete with sophisticated hypocaust installations.

Although used as a quarry for masonry during the Ottoman period, enough remains of Pliska to give a coherent picture of its architectural evolution and the splendour of its heyday. Pliska began life as an armed encampments for the Bulgar warriors and their families who lived in leather *yurts* (Central Asian nomads' tents). A stone model of such a yurt, preserved in the Varna Archaeological Museum, is engraved with a hunting scene, indicating that the outer walls of these yurts were often painted. The original outer defences of Pliska consisted of a ditch with an earthwork behind it, surmounted by a wooden palisade.

Plates 6–8

As Pliska grew in size and importance, the public buildings of the khan and the city ramparts took on a more monumental appearance. Within the outer earthworks was erected a massive inner wall of immense limestone blocks, with round corner-bastions, crenellated battlements, and pentagonal towers set at intervals. The four gate-houses were impressive structures of immense strength.

Inside these inner ramparts was a third set of walls, this time of brick, enclosing the khan's personal residence. The original palace buildings had brick walls erected on stone foundations, and wooden balconies. Byzantine chroniclers record that the soldiers of the Byzantine emperor Nicephorus set fire to these and destroyed them during the invasion of 811, in the course of which Nicephorus perished. The buildings were

Plates 7, 8

reconstructed on a grander scale by Khan Omurtag, whose Large Palace was a magnificent two-storey structure of limestone ashlar blocks, surrounded by a stone pavement. The throne room was 30 metres long. What is left of the palace complex shows that it also included two rectangular, almost square chambers, which are built concentrically. Here are clearly the remains of an imperial sanctuary or pagan temple, such as are also found at Madara and at Preslav. Precisely which pagan gods were worshipped here is not known, though Professor B. Brentjes may well be right in saying that we must look for the prototype in Central Asia, notably in the Parthian-Kushan region. Whether the cult practised here was that of the supreme god of the early Turkic peoples, *Tengri* or *Tangra*, creator of the world, or alternatively that of Buddhism, as Brentjes suggests, remains debatable.

Along the ceremonial avenues leading to the khans' palace, were erected rows of statues and ornamented columns, many of them looted by Khan Krum from the imperial villas and palaces of Constantinople.

SHUMEN

Pliska was not the only important architectural monument of the pagan Bulgar khans. At Madara, close to the Horseman relief, are extensive remains of fortified buildings, as well as those of the pagan temple.

Also of great interest are the proto-Bulgar fortifications at Shumen castle, commanding the passes leading to Pliska and Preslav. Here too are impressive walls and forts from the Thracian and Roman periods, later enlarged and improved by Emperor Justinian in the sixth century. The Greeks refer to Shumen as 'Symeon', of which 'Shumen' is a popular corruption.

The proto-Bulgar ramparts at Shumen, like those in Pliska, are set with pentagonal and round bastions. The inner citadel was roofed with large beams. On my visit in 1971, during excavations carried out by Vera Antonova, I saw an inscription in Greek letters, encrusted and picked out with reddish paint (like the Madara inscriptions), mentioning a certain Ostron Bogoyin, probably a governor during the reign of Khan Tervel (701–18). When Emperor Nicephorus destroyed Pliska in 811, he failed to take Shumen, which was then used temporarily as a capital by Khan Krum. Princess Anna Comnena describes a military expedition to Shumen, undertaken by Emperor Alexius Comnenus (1081–1118), and says that the castle was known locally as 'the Scythian

Parliament House', no doubt because it was a place where popular assemblies were held.

In the Shumen Archaeological Museum can be seen a reconstruction of the Aul of Omurtag, which was a fortified cavalry barracks, with strong brick walls, built in 822, and mentioned in the proto-Bulgar inscription of Chatalar. Inside the aul were stables and living quarters for Khan Omurtag's picked cavalry brigade. This is a most interesting example of proto-Bulgar military architecture.

Also at Shumen are preserved specimens of pagan Slavonic 'kamen-nye baby'. These are massive stone idols, of female form, about 2½ metres high; they were originally set up in vertical position, the bottom half-metre length being buried in the ground. Crude in execution, these forbidding stone figures are also found extensively in South Russia. They are embodiments of Slavonic pagan fertility cults, and symbolize matriarchal authority in the tribe.

Fig. 4

Carved high up on the cliff at Madara, almost within sight of Pliska, is THE MADARA the impressive figure of the Madara Horseman. This relief depicts an HORSEMAN equestrian Great Khan of the Bulgars; he holds the reins in his right hand and a wine cup in his left. The horse is trampling on a lion, while Plates 4, 5 behind it there runs an agile greyhound.

The height of the relief, including the rider himself, is almost 3 metres; the carving is more than 25 metres above ground level. To make the figures stand out better from a distance, the master-carver picked them out with red plaster, traces of which may still be seen on the horse's body. Red plaster was also used to fill in the letters of the three important Greek historical inscriptions alongside the Horseman. These record important events of Bulgarian history during the eighth and early ninth centuries, and are the earliest Bulgarian historical documents yet found.

This figure was undoubtedly intended to symbolize the imperial might of the early Bulgar khans. The obvious parallels are the reliefs of the palace at Persepolis and on the near-by cliffs of Naqsh-i-Rustam, in Iran, where we see carved in the living rock a whole cycle of historical events involving Persian royal figures. The Parthian bas-reliefs of Tang-i-Sarwak also spring to mind. Further interesting comparisons may be drawn with the three Central Asian Buddhist paintings, more or less contemporary with the Madara Horseman, showing a rider king with cup in hand. (These were described by Dr Emel Esin in a lecture delivered at the School of Oriental and African Studies, London, on 29 May 1974.) Looking forward in time, we may recall moreover that the Sultan on horseback was a favourite theme of Seljuq art in Anatolia, and then of the Mongols in the thirteenth century. Both of these peoples, of course, had a certain ethnic affinity with the proto-Bulgars.

METALWORK
AND
CERAMICS

From the seventh to the tenth century, there flourished in South Russia, and around the Carpathians, a school of metalworkers who are usually likened to the Sasanian silver-workers of Iran. At the same time, a brilliant, hybrid style was developed by the Gepids in the territory of modern Romania. The proto-Bulgars drew much inspiration from these schools, as may be seen from the important set of gold vessels forming the Treasure of Nagy Sankt Miklós.

Plates 12-16

Now preserved in the Vienna Kunsthistorisches Museum, the Treasure was accidentally discovered in 1799 in a village in the Roman-ian Banat, which formed part of the First Bulgarian Empire from 804 to 896. It comprises twenty-three vessels: seven ewers, one fruit dish, four small bowls, two cups, one rhyton, one larger bowl, four goblets, and three unusual bowls with animal heads. The lively and imaginative decoration of the Treasure is truly remarkable; on some of the ewers, a highly eclectic composition has been achieved. Some motifs are of Byzantine and Classical Greek inspiration, while elsewhere we find Oriental deities, such as the goddess Anahita. A medallion portraying a ruler riding an anthropoid ape points to the influence of totemistic legends connected with the origin of the Turkic peoples. An element of topicality is provided by a medallion showing a rider, entirely dressed in a coat of mail, dragging a captive along by the hair, while the head of a slain enemy hangs from the saddle of his horse. This must be one of the earliest portrayals of a warrior in a coat of mail, since this type of armour first appeared in Europe in the ninth century. The Bulgarian proven-ance of the Nagy Sankt Miklós Treasure is confirmed by the Christian liturgical inscriptions engraved on the vessels, including also the Bulgar titles of rank *boïlya* and *zhupan*.

The interaction of Slavonic and proto-Bulgar traditions is well seen in the case of pottery. The Slavs had rather uninspiring cooking pots, both hand-made and wheel-turned, and often ornamented with wavy

Fig. 6

lines, such as those from Popina illustrated by Marija Gimbutas in her book on the Slavs. The proto-Bulgars introduced into the Balkans many of the old artistic traditions and techniques from the northern regions of the Black Sea and the Caucasus. They made vessels with one or two handles, ewers with necks curved like those of birds, and small amphora-like water-jugs. Their surfaces were often entirely glazed, or ornamented with polished stripes, vertical or else crossed to form a net-work. The proto-Bulgars also had markedly elongated, bottle-shaped water-jugs, glazed in green; on their sides or base they have special signs, identical with those stamped on bricks and tiles used in buildings of the proto-Bulgar period.

Plates 10, 11

The adoption of Christianity by Prince Boris-Michael in 864/65 led to a rapid change in cultural orientation, which had profound effects on the evolution of architecture and art throughout Bulgaria. One of the first manifestations of this new era was the erection at Pliska, alongside the massive fortifications of the pagan Bulgars, of an enormous cathedral church, a superb example of the Christian basilica.

EARLY
CHRISTIAN
ARCHITEC-
TURE

Christian architecture was, of course, not a complete innovation in Bulgaria; the whole country was dotted with the remains of early Christian sanctuaries, dating from the period between the fourth and sixth centuries. Most of these had been destroyed by the invading Slavs and by the pagan proto-Bulgars.

By the time of Boris-Michael, the art of building domed churches was perfectly well understood in Byzantium, as we know from the example of Saint Sophia in Constantinople, dating from the sixth century. Further refinements in construction of domes were made by the Armen-ians in the seventh century, and these were widely applied throughout Byzantium.

The basilica was a precursor of the domed church, and as an archi-tectural form may thus be considered more archaic. Essentially it is a simple, even barn-shaped structure, a temple without a dome, and early pagan examples may be found in various parts of the Roman Empire. However, the form is capable of great elaboration, and is also easier and quicker to build than a domed church, especially when a very large and imposing building was required in a hurry, as at Pliska. Boris-Michael's architects could well have used as one of their models

Fig. 28 Some medieval cultural centres of Bulgaria and Macedonia. (After Weitzman and others)

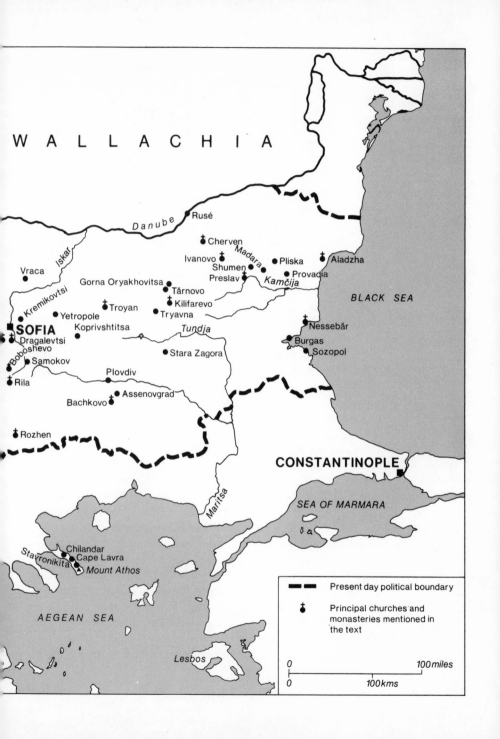

WALLACHIA

Danube • Rusé

♀ Cherven

Ivanovo ♀ Madara • Pliska ♀ Aladzha

Shumen
Vraca • Preslav *Kamčija* • Provadia

Gorna Oryakhovitsa BLACK SEA

Iskar Tărnovo

Kremikovtsi ♀ Troyan ♀ Kilifarevo

Yetropole Tryavna

■ SOFIA Koprivshtitsa *Tundja* ♀ Nessebăr

Dragalevtsi

Boboshevo • Burgas

♀ Samokov • Stara Zagora • Sozopol

♀ Rila Plovdiv

Bachkovo ♀ • Assenovgrad

♀ Rozhen

CONSTANTINOPLE ■

Maritsa SEA OF MARMARA

Chilandar
Stavronikita • Cape Lavra

Mount Athos

AEGEAN SEA

Lesbos

━ ━ Present day political boundary

♀ Principal churches and
monasteries mentioned in
the text

0 _____ 100 miles
0 _____ 100 kms

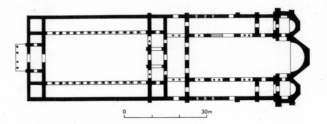

Fig. 29 Pliska. The Great Basilica of Prince Boris-Michael. Ground plan. (After Dimitrov and others)

Fig. 29

Fig. 32

the basilica of St Demetrius in Thessalonica, rebuilt in the seventh century; this was a city with which the Bulgarians had regular commercial links. Also relevant for purposes of comparison is the ruined metropolitan basilica at Nessebăr (Mesembria), dated by some as early as the fifth century, though André Grabar attributes it to the ninth.

The royal basilica at Pliska is not only the biggest building dating from the early Christian period in Bulgaria, but also the largest church built anywhere at that period. It is 99 metres long, if we count the cloistered forecourt or atrium, and almost 30 metres wide. It introduces the characteristic Byzantine style of construction using alternate courses of brick and stone, rather than massive ashlar blocks alone, as in pagan times. The interior of the cathedral contains a nave and two aisles; broad pilasters alternate with marble columns with carved capitals to form colonnades separating the aisles from the central area. There were galleries above the aisles and the narthex, and down below, special seats for the heads of the State and Church hierarchy. Four sarcophagi containing the mortal remains of Bulgar nobles were discovered in the ruins in 1970.

Following the abdication of Boris-Michael, and the accession of Tsar Symeon in 893, the royal residence was moved from Pliska, with its pagan associations, to a new site at Great Preslav, also in the region of the modern town of Shumen. There Tsar Symeon built himself a magnificent palace, the foundations of which measure 30 by 25 metres. A huge column of green breccia stone, now re-erected on the spot where it originally stood, indicates the height of the building, which inherited the monumental size that characterized the pagan palaces of Pliska. Full advantage was taken of the sloping terrain to erect portions of the palace at different levels, so that they did not screen one another, but rather lent variety to the whole ensemble. Numerous decorative plaques and fragments of sculptured marble plinths and friezes, remains of multi-

128

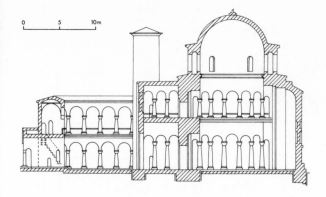

Fig. 30 Great Preslav. Golden or Round Church of Tsar Symeon, early tenth century. Sectional elevation (After Hoddinott)

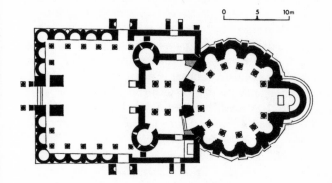

Fig. 31 Great Preslav. Golden or Round Church of Tsar Symeon. Ground plan (After Bichev)

coloured floor mosaics, and wall facings made of glazed and painted pottery, indicate the luxurious standard to which the palace was designed and finished, while the many water pipes and drains show that plumbing and sanitation were not neglected. Among the carved decorations encountered on door frames and other prominent places are lions and other beasts, griffins of the Persian type, as well as the palmetto in heart-shaped frame often met with in buildings from Constantinople. The taste for such carvings was in due course to spread to other centres such as Stara Zagora.

Plates 23, 24

Associated with the royal palace was the magnificent Golden or Round Church at Great Preslav, erected by Symeon early in the tenth century. The three parts of the church – the rotunda with its twelve columns, the narthex flanked by round towers, and the atrium with its

Plates 19, 20, Figs. 30, 31

Fig. 32 Fragments of marble decoration from the royal palace and Round Church at Preslav. In one example (left), oblong and lozenge-shaped enamel and coloured ceramic inlay incrustations were let into the marble, producing a polychrome effect. (After Hensel)

colonnade – are blended with a fine sense of proportion, and show a harmonious interplay of line and space. The British scholar R. F. Hoddinott has drawn interesting parallels with the palatine church of Charlemagne at Aachen. As in the Preslav palace, the standard of decoration was of the highest. The dome was gilded, and shone for miles around. On the walls, glazed pottery tiles of circular, square, rectangular or diamond shape gleamed, while even the floor was laid with pottery incrustations.

Figs. 34, 35

There are many other buildings of great interest dating from the era of Tsar Symeon. A good example is Vinitsa church – a small domed building of the 'apse-buttressed' square type, in which the polygonal cupola is suspended upon the central square area without the aid of free-standing piers. This is achieved by the skilful use of squinches, as evolved in Georgia and Armenia at such monuments as Jvari church close to Mtskheta (early seventh century) and St Hripsimé in Echmiadzin (AD 618). Dr S. Boyadjiev has drawn interesting parallels between Vinitsa and the Georgian churches of Kumurdo and Nikordsminda, which date from the tenth and the eleventh century respectively. Furthermore, Vinitsa's elegant blind arcading on the original structure suggests Caucasian affinities.

Fig. 33 Great Preslav. Two small domed churches of the period of Tsar Symeon. Ground plans. (After Dimitrov and others)

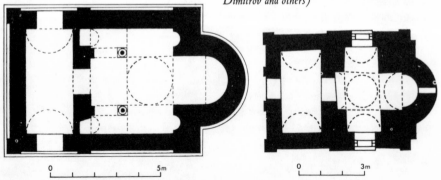

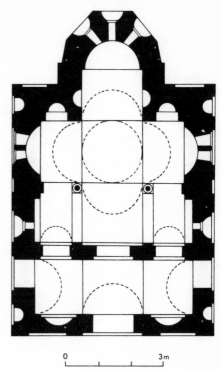

Fig. 34 Vinitsa church: reconstruction of the west façade. (After Boyadjiev)

Fig. 35 Vinitsa church: ground plan of the original edifice. (After Boyadjiev)

0 — 3m

For 167 years, from 1018 to 1185, Bulgaria was incorporated into the Byzantine Empire. Hence church architecture tended to copy familiar Greek provincial patterns. Also, there was little scope for grand palaces and cathedrals on the pattern of Preslav, since political power and wealth were now centred in the Byzantine emperor at Constantinople.

The period of Byzantine supremacy in Bulgaria was marked by a growth of monastic life, partly under the impulse of Mount Athos, the monasteries of which were easily reached from Bulgaria by crossing the Rhodope range. From the reign of Alexius Comnenus, in the year 1083, dates the establishment of the important monastery of Bachkovo, to the south of Assenovgrad. The founders were a Byzantine general of Armeno‹Georgian descent, Gregory Bakuriani, and his brother Abasi, and the monastery was reserved exclusively for monks of Georgian nationality. The general layout and grouping of the monastery buildings certainly recalls such Caucasian foundations as Haghpat and

Plate 28

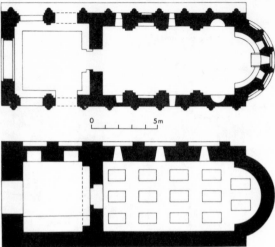

Fig. 36 Bachkovo monastery: the ossuary or mausoleum. Ground plans of the upper and lower levels. (After Dimitrov and others)

0   5 m

Fig. 36

Sanahin in northern Armenia, and Gelati in western Georgia, all of which date from this era. Particularly striking at Bachkovo is the ossuary or funeral church, which lies more than two hundred yards outside the main complex. Of basilican outline, the ossuary is built on two levels, the upper storey being a single-nave chapel for the holding of funeral and memorial services, and the lower storey or crypt containing fourteen spaces for graves. Similar edifices were common in Armenia from the eleventh century onwards, especially in Siunia province. Of the other original Bachkovo buildings, only the twelfth-century church of the Holy Archangels survives, the rest having been destroyed by the Turks in the fifteenth century. Thus, the central church with its impressive dome dates from the seventeenth century, while the refectory with its magnificent frescoes is dated 1606.

Plates 25–27

Even better known than Bachkovo is the Rila monastery situated in the Rila Mountains to the south of Sofia. This shrine, close to the original hermitage of St John of Rila, has been a favourite place of pilgrimage from the early Middle Ages to the present day. Owing to a great fire in 1833, little remains of the medieval buildings apart from a bastion known as Khrelyo's Tower. This fortified stronghold dates from 1335, and was erected by a retired Bulgarian notable, the Caesar Stefan Khrelyo Dragovol, who retired to Rila to escape from the world and from his enemies. Khrelyo also built one of the monastery churches, now

132

destroyed, but his career was cut short when he was murdered in 1342. The importance of Rila monastery during the Second Bulgarian Empire is shown by many relics in the Rila Museum, including a chrysobull or royal golden charter of Tsar Ivan Shishman, dated 1378. Notable features of the modern buildings, erected from 1834 onwards, are splendid carved wooden ceilings, and a cycle of highly realistic murals painted by the Bulgarian master-painter of the nineteenth century, Zakhari Zograf.

Plates 43, 44

In spite of the depredations of the Turks, Bulgaria is studded with many other magnificent monasteries. We may single out the Preo-brazhenski monastery near Great Tărnovo, founded by Tsar Ivan Alexander, and rebuilt in the nineteenth century by that self-taught genius, Kolyo Ficheto, who also constructed dozens of handsome bridges, public buildings and other monuments; the Troyan monastery, situated to the north of an important pass over the Balkan range, and renowned for its special brand of *Slivova* or plum brandy liqueur; and the Rozhen monastery, five miles from the town of Melnik near the Greek frontier. The Rozhen monastery, which had special links with the Iviron or Georgian monastery on Mount Athos, has fine frescoes and icons as well as picturesque and grotesque wood carvings of the seven-teenth century.

Plates 58, 59

Besides the monasteries, church building also contained apace, both during the Byzantine dominance, and under the Second Bulgarian Empire, up to 1393. We can distinguish several categories of church: the simple village church, the fortified castle-church, and the more opulent city churches encountered at Tărnovo, at Nessebăr, and else-where. The castle-church is well exemplified by the twelfth-century domed church of the Petrich Virgin, at Assenova Krepost (Assen's Castle), not far from the Bachkovo monastery; it has two storeys, and a massive tower at one end, surmounted by a belfry.

Plate 29,
Fig. 37

Owing to wholesale Turkish destruction of the seventeen churches of the Bulgarian royal family and of leading nobles grouped on the Trapezitsa hill at Tărnovo, we can now judge the splendour of thirteenth- and fourteenth-century Bulgarian architecture only by visiting the port of Nessebăr (Mesembria), which enjoyed a remarkable economic and cultural upswing during this period. Apart from the elegant basilica of St Parasceva, the fourteenth-century churches are fine examples of the

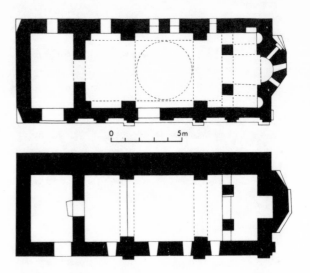

Fig. 37 Church of the Petrich Virgin, at Assenova Krepost. Built on two storeys, the church has a massive tower and belfry at the west end. Ground plan of upper and lower levels. (After Dimitrov and others)

Palaeologan style of cubic building, in the form of an inscribed cross and central dome, usually with other subsidiary domes. The Pantocrator and the Archangels each have their own tower, as at Mistra near Sparta.

The façades are beautifully decorated with niches, the red of the bricks alternating with the bright colour of the dressed stone. Rows of discs and quatrefoil rosettes in green-glazed red ceramic complete the décor. On a visit to Nessebăr in 1971, I was shown the technique by which these ceramic decorations were originally set into the wall: the visible part of the discs and rosettes is backed by a plug rather like an egg-cup or a pie funnel, which can be pushed firmly into soft mortar. When the sun shines upon these patterns of green-glazed insets the effect is very fine indeed. In the opinion of Professor André Grabar: 'Three churches at Mesembria – St John-Aliturgitos, the Pantocrator and the Archangels – are as fine as the best ecclesiastical architecture of the fourteenth century in Thessalonica and Mistra.'

Plate 32,
Fig. 38

The insecurity of life prevailing in medieval Bulgaria encouraged the growth of monasteries and churches carved out of remote cliff-sides, as it did in Cappadocia and medieval Georgia. A famous example is the Aladzha monastery, two miles southwest of the resort of Golden Sands, near Varna, which features two chapels, also cells, catacombs and rock-cut tombs, some dating from the thirteenth and fourteenth centuries.

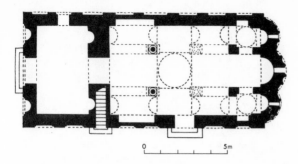

Plates 39-42

Fig. 38 Nessebăr: Pantocrator church, thirteenth-fourteenth century. Ground plan. (After Dimitrov and others)

Originally the monastery was decorated with beautiful wall-paintings; but in the words of Professor Charles Veyrenc, 'thoughtless visitors damaged the frescoes, which but for this would be among the finest works of the Middle Ages, in Bulgaria.' Also of great interest is the rock-cut church at Ivanovo in the deeply eroded gorges of the river Rusenski Lom, a tributary of the Danube. Here also we have the sad remains of magnificent frescoes of the fourteenth-century Tărnovo school.

The restoration of Bulgarian independence under the Assen dynasty brought to Great Tărnovo two centuries of picturesque splendour, prior to the Ottoman conquest of 1393. However, the Second Bulgarian Empire was a more fragile, insecure entity than the First. The massive and self-confident style of Pliska and Preslav is lacking, and the tsar himself was obliged to take up his residence on a lofty hill overlooking the river Yantra, protected from foes by ramparts and portcullis gates.

SECULAR ARCHITEC-TURE

Between my first and third visits to Tărnovo, in 1967 and 1971 respectively, great progress was already being made in excavating and reconstructing the Tsarevets or acropolis of Tărnovo. This remarkable complex of buildings, once the metropolis of the Balkan peninsula, has many features recalling the medieval Tower of London, since it served as royal residence, stronghold, state prison, as well as being the administrative centre for the surrounding city. Many merchants' and workers' houses have been excavated. The townsfolk lived in small square two-storey houses, with roofs tiled with thin rectangular slabs of stone, as used in Bulgaria to this day; the serfs in primitive dug-outs of wattle and mud. The patriarch's palace, on the other hand, was a splendid edifice, and stood higher than that of the tsar, perhaps to emphasize the tsar's role as 'Defender of the Faith'. Among the impressive medieval fortifications there stands out the so-called Baldwin's Tower, where the

Fig. 16

Latin emperor of that name is said to have been imprisoned after his defeat by the Bulgarians in 1205. (The manner of Baldwin's death is obscure: Tsar Kaloyan wrote to Pope Innocent III that Baldwin had died in prison; but one contemporary says that his hands and feet were cut off and he was hurled into a ravine, where he died on the third day.)

Plate 33

The Baba Vida castle towers at Vidin, on the right bank of the Danube, constitute another noteworthy monument. Probably dating back to the thirteenth century, this magnificent castle was several times rebuilt under Ottoman domination; it is the only ancient Bulgarian fortress to survive in anything resembling its medieval form.

While I was staying at Varna in 1971, the local archaeologist Alexander Kuzov took me to see the remains of the citadel near the town of Provadia, otherwise called Ovech. This citadel, named Ovechgrad, stands high above the town; it was approached by a rocky ridge, artificially cut away so as to isolate the stronghold, which was entered only by a drawbridge, 7 metres long. The castle entry was arched over with stone, and a tower built above. The south end of the fortress was guarded by two square corner-bastions. Water supply presented a great problem, as there was no stream or spring. Rain-water was collected in large rock-cut cisterns, and there was a great well 73 metres deep, as we learn from the Turkish traveller Evliya Chelebi.

Fig. 39

From a later period, special interest attaches to the square fortified mansions at Bansko, and also at the village of Arbanassi, near Tărnovo. Many of these massive houses date from the seventeenth century, and each was inhabited by a whole clan of warlike villagers or merchants, prepared to defend their lives against marauding Turks and outlaws. The familiar Balkan veranda'd houses with pitched roof and individual

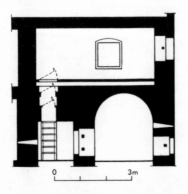

Fig. 39 Bansko. The Hadjigiorgov fortified house. Sectional diagram showing winter quarters and refuge room. (After Dimitrov and others)

garden, so characteristic of Tărnovo, Koprivshtitsa and other towns, date mainly from the eighteenth and nineteenth centuries.

One of the arts for which the Bulgarians, ancient and modern, have always shown a natural aptitude, is that of wood-carving. Two fine examples from our period are the twelfth-century door of St Nicholas' church in Ohrida, carved with warrior saints and fantastic beasts, and the fourteenth-century wooden door from Khrelyo's Tower, now in the Rila Museum. Also to be seen at Rila is the magnificent decorated ceiling of the Koprivshtitsa Room and several superb iconostases or altar screens (paralleled in a number of other Bulgarian churches and monasteries).

WOOD-
CARVING

Plate 51

So devoted were the Rila craftsmen to their wood-carving that a certain Monk Raphael spent twelve years, from 1790 to 1802, in fashioning a wonderful decorated cross, using tiny implements including an ordinary pin, as a result of which he became blind.

Among leading Bulgarian schools of wood-carving are those of Samokov and Razlog, both not far from Rila. During the Bulgarian renaissance of the nineteenth century, prominence was attained by the Tryavna school, centred on the little mountain town of that name.

The master carpenters, builders and wood-carvers of Tryavna roamed the entire Ottoman Empire in search of work, and records concerning them go back to the year 1804. They fashioned iconostases, crosses, altars, thrones, and icons; their work shows a fine feeling for line, and is imbued with vibrance and power. Their mastery is well shown in the carved ceiling at the Daskalov house, in Tryavna itself. The remarkable wood carvings on the iconostasis at Rozhen monastery, dating from the seventeenth century, have been mentioned earlier.

Plate 57
Plates 58, 59

All this elegance and originality spilt over into more homely articles, including kitchen utensils, children's toys, and agricultural implements. These wooden objects have a long history of evolution behind them, though few medieval examples have survived the ravages of time. However, scenes on frescoes, such as those preserved in the Tărnovo Historical Museum, and also some of the actual exhibits there, combine to give us a good idea of the beautifully carved objects in use in medieval Bulgaria, ranging from musical instruments to sophisticated items of furniture – chairs, tables, benches, and royal thrones.

The Bulgarians

Fresco and mural painting has a long and distinguished history in Bulgaria, going back to Thracian times, as we know from the world-famous painted tomb at Kazanluk. The introduction, or rather, revival of Christianity in Bulgaria in the ninth century provided a strong stimulus for the art of the mural painter, and the local artists were not slow to respond to this. Even though the frescoes in medieval Bulgarian churches follow certain established patterns, notably the icono-graphic system introduced by the patriarchal authority in Constanti-nople and finalized in the eleventh century, the Bulgarian masters nevertheless felt free to introduce many naturalistic touches of their own. While it may be too much to speak of a well-defined 'national style' in the period under review, it must be said that the Bulgarian painters show a delightful ability to blend the divine and the human element in pleasing harmony. They are masters of delicate and striking colours, and contrive to avoid the stylized coldness characteristic of so much of the art of the Byzantine capital during this period.

Among the earliest extant examples we can cite the eleventh-century murals in the church of St Sophia in Ohrida, which are distinguished by pronounced archaic features. The Fathers of the Church depicted here, including St John Chrysostom, are seen often in motionless icon-like poses, with massive forms, and head modelled in sharp con-trast of light and shade. The austere hues employed heighten the virile element in the portrayal of these hieratic figures.

Plate 35

Nearly nine centuries in the history of Bulgarian fresco-painting can be traced by visiting the Bachkovo monastery. The ossuary or funeral chapel has a set of murals dating from the eleventh and twelfth centuries, including a sublime portrayal of the Holy Virgin; also gaunt hermits with dishevelled hair and a fanatical gleam in their eyes, scenes from Christ's life, the Last Judgement, and many other figures and scenes. The Bachkovo monastery's connection with Georgia is stressed by the inclusion of figures of Saints Euthymius and George, both of whom were abbots of the Iviron monastery on Mount Athos. As Mrs Elka Bakalova justly remarks, 'we cannot fail to admire the antique harmony, classic finesse, lucidity and balance of the murals, the plastic forms of some of the faces, which reveal great spiritual qualities.' Also on view at Bachkovo are the frescoes of the refectory in the Salonica style, dating from 1630, and restored in 1970–71 by the Czech master Raimund Ondráček, in whose company I inspected them on the spot. Finally, the monastery churches of the Archangels and of St Nicholas were further embellished by the illustrious Zakhari Zograf in 1840–41, his paintings evoking the whole world of Bulgarian religious and national consciousness during the period of renascence.

Plates 43, 44

The highest achievement of monumental painting under the Second Bulgarian Empire is usually considered to be the set of murals in the church of Boyana village, a suburb of Sofia. This interesting building was built in two stages, and has two superimposed sets of murals – the first dating from the Comnenian period, around 1100. The earlier master used a light tone in his paintings, with abstract celestial figures, painted with long smooth lines and large flat areas of transparent whites, light greens, pinks and blue against a light-blue background. In 1259, on the orders of Kaloyan, the local feudal magnate or *sebastocrator*, the Boyana church was enlarged and fresh murals were executed by anonymous artists, whose work embodied the best features of the then flourishing Tărnovo school. These artists displayed great creative audacity in the arrangement of traditional figures, and in the composition of ensemble effects. The tableaux illustrating the life of Christ are painted with rich imagination and a fine feeling for space, colour and linear rhythm. Many of the scenes contain details drawn from the life of the Bulgarian people at that time, for instance the bunches of garlic which figure in the Last Supper; whereas the harmonious poses and folds in the garments, which we see in the Annunciation, were inspired by Antiquity. Excellent examples of medieval Bulgarian portraiture are the figures of Tsar Constantine Assen Tikh and his first consort, Queen Irina; in particular, those of the donors Sebastocrator Kaloyan and his wife Dessislava. These are speaking likenesses, of the greatest individuality and beauty.

Plates 36–38

Fig. 17
Fig. 40

During the fourteenth century, the era of Tsar Ivan Alexander saw a glorious late flowering of Bulgarian Christian art of the Second Empire. Dating from this period are about a dozen attractive churches with painted walls. These include the church of St Peter at Berendé; the rock-cut chapel at Ivanovo, above the river Rusenski Lom, St Theodore at Boboshevo; the church of SS Peter and Paul at Tărnovo; and the much admired church of St John the Theologian at Zemen monastery, between Sofia and Kyustendil. At Zemen, the cycle of Our Lord's

Plates 39–42
Fig. 41

Fig. 40 The Sebastocrator Kaloyan and his wife, Princess Dessislava. Donor portraits in Boyana church near Sofia (1259). Kaloyan wears formal dress, with a dark green mantle, dark blue shoes, and a coronet with a green emerald in front; Dessislava's dalmatic has pairs of heraldic lions symmetrically grouped round the Tree of Life. (After Naslednikova)

Crucifixion is executed in masterly fashion, with a curiously stylized portrayal of the sleepy Disciples trying to stay awake and pray on the Mount of Olives, and a strikingly villainous Jewish mob coming out to seize Jesus; the figures include impressive martyrs and warrior saints. At Boboshevo, the traitor Judas Iscariot hangs ignominiously from a tree. Here and there in this group, we see stylized and elongated human figures, curved into an 'S' shape; the portrayal of the naked body is not unknown, and there is a wide variety of pose and movement.

Strangely enough, even the Turkish oppression could not stem the inventiveness of the Bulgarian mural painters. The Dragalevtsi monastery near Sofia has beautiful frescoes of the fifteenth century, as do also those at Kremikovtsi and Poganovo. Fine seventeenth-century frescoes are to be found at Arbanassi near Tărnovo, even though the churches them-selves had to be built half down into the ground to avoid offending Turkish susceptibilities. The church of the Nativity there contains a portrayal of the Bulgarian *khoro* or round dance. Arbanassi also boasts a spectacular representation of an oecumenical council in session at Constantinople.

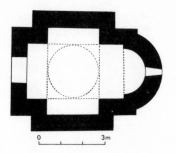

Fig. 41 Boboshevo. Ruined cruciform church of St Theodore. Originally built in the eleventh or twelfth century, the church has renowned fresco paintings of the fourteenth. Ground plan. (After Dimitrov and others)

Closely linked with the ritual of the Eastern Orthodox Church, the icon has always been venerated by the Christian Bulgarians as an especially sacred object. For centuries, icons have been the goal of pilgrimages, have taken part in religious processions, led armies into battle, borne witness to court ceremonies and coronations of kings and potentates, graced convivial gatherings on the christening of a new-born child, or helped to pay final homage to the departed. Moreover, the icons of Bulgaria express the inspiration of talented artists who, though working within the framework of a canonized and stylized art-form, have left the imprint of highly individual creative work.

The oldest known Bulgarian icon is something of a curiosity; it is an image of St Theodore made up of twenty square glazed ceramic tiles, the basic colours being gold, light brown and greenish black. Discovered at Patleina near Preslav in 1909, this work is a product of the ceramic workshop set up by Tsar Symeon about the year 900, with a view to embellishing his palace and churches at Preslav.

Plate 45

Literary texts of the period bear witness to the popularity of icons in Bulgaria towards the end of the First Empire. John the Exarch translated into Bulgarian the treatise on icons written by St John Damascene. Around AD 970 Cosmas the Priest, fulminating against the Bogomil heretics, exclaims:

> Whoever fails to kiss with love and awe the icons of Our Lord or His Mother and all the Saints, may he be damned! . . . And when we behold on an icon the blessed Mother of God, then we cry out from the very depths of our hearts: Most Holy Mother of God, forget not thy children! . . . When we behold on an icon Christ's lovable

image clasped in thine arms, then do we sinners rejoice, sink to our knees, and kiss Him with adoration.

Already in the time of Cosmas images of individual saints, painted in bright colours on wooden panels or boards, were in existence; for he goes on to say: 'The evil spirits quake in fear before the image of the Lord painted on a board . . . We do not bow before the paint or the wood but rather before Him who is portrayed thereon.'

The Byzantine chronicler Leo the Deacon says that when Emperor John Tzimiskes sacked Preslav in 972, he found there an icon of the Odegitria Virgin, which he ceremoniously carried off to Constantinople. The Odegitria Virgin and Child was a favourite subject of medieval Bulgarians and Serbian iconpainters; many of the finest examples are fitted with a chased repoussé silver or silver gilt casing or frame ('oklad'), producing a nimbate effect.

As we move into the later Middle Ages, a whole series of icons, painted in tempera upon wood, bear witness to the artistic talent and technical maturity of the Bulgarian masters. The best of these can be seen in the special exhibition in the crypt of the St Alexander Nevsky Cathedral, the Archaeological Museum, and the Central Ecclesiastical Museum, all in Sofia, and in various monastery collections and provincial museums. A famous icon of the Tărnovo period, known as the 'Christ Untouched by Human Hands', has found its way to Laon, in France.

Plates 46, 47

From surviving icon masterpieces antedating the Turkish conquest of 1393–96, we may cite the noble 'Annunciation' from St Clement's church in Ohrida, a work of the eleventh or twelfth century (illustrated by Bogdan Filov in his *L'Ancien Art Bulgare*); the unusual 'St George Crowned and Enthroned' from the Plovdiv region, dating from the end of the thirteenth century; the fourteenthcentury Virgin Eleusa, from Nessebăr; the doublesided icon of the Virgin and St John the Theologian, from the Poganovo monastery, dated about 1390; and the 'Crucifixion' from Bulgarovo, dating probably from the fourteenth century (all four of the lastnamed are reproduced in Svetlin Bossilkov's *Twelve Icons from Bulgaria*, the 'St George' in colour). Superb technique and exquisite colours characterize every one of these splendid pieces. It is interesting that one of the most venerated of Bulgarian icons, the miracle working Virgin of Bachkovo, has an inscription in Georgian recording that it was presented to the monastery in 1311 by two Georgian brothers.

The earliest surviving Glagolitic and Cyrillic manuscripts copied in Bulgaria, dating from the tenth century onwards, were strictly plain, utilitarian productions; apart from modestly decorated capital letters, the scribes indulged their artistic fancy very little. A great advance is notice´ able from the reign of Tsar Ivan Assen II (1218–41) onwards. From this period date the illuminated Gospels of the Priest Dobreisho, con´ taining full´page figures of the four Apostles. In their delightfully naive imagery and striking colouring, these appear like distant cousins of the figures in such archaic Celtic manuscripts as the Book of Kells.

An altogether more sophisticated style is seen in two famous monu´ ments of the age of Tsar Ivan Alexander, in the fourteenth century. The first of these is the Slavonic recension of the Byzantine chronicle or 'Historical Synopsis' of Constantine Manasses (d. 1187), copied in 1344–45, and now in the Vatican Library; the other is the personal Gospel book of Tsar Ivan Alexander, copied in 1355–56 by the Monk Symeon, and brought to England in 1837 from Mount Athos by Robert Curzon. Also pertaining to this group is the richly decorated Tomich Psalter, now in Moscow, and the slightly later Radomir Psalter with its remarkable plant and animal figures.

Thanks to the efforts of Professor Ivan Duichev of Sofia University, the Slavonic Manasses chronicle was published in a monochrome facsimile edition in 1963; the complete series of miniatures in colour appeared at Sofia in 1965. Most of the sixty´nine miniatures in the text Plate 49 were 're´edited' by the illustrator from lost Greek models. More than a score are original and vivid treatments of episodes in Bulgarian history, particularly the great battles of the reigns of Khan Krum and Tsar Samuel. Among the episodes illustrated is that of Khan Krum drinking out of the skull of the slain Emperor Nicephorus, and then being routed by Emperor Leo the Armenian. Elsewhere we see the Russians under Svyatoslav attacking Bulgaria in 969, and later being defeated by Emperor John Tzimiskes. All these miniatures are of interest for study of architecture, military life and court ceremonial under the Bulgarian khans and tsars. The colouring remains bright to this day, and the sense of lively movement and dramatic action is pronounced.

The Gospels of Tsar Alexander are on permanent exhibition in the British Museum. This parchment codex is noted for the extensive series of 366 miniatures illustrating the main episodes of all four Gospels. The cycle of illustrations is derived from a Byzantine traditional prototype, of which a famous example is the eleventh-century Greek Gospel Book, manuscript No. 74 in the Bibliothèque Nationale in Paris. The entire cycle of Bulgarian miniatures was published in Sofia by Bogdan Filov in 1934. Among the many curious features created by the Bulgarian artist's imagination is the clothing of the resurrected Lazarus in the robes of an Orthodox bishop! Of special interest for Bulgarian history are the magnificent full-length portraits of Tsar Ivan Alexander and his family, attired in gold, scarlet and purple robes. In order to please his royal client, the illustrator shows Ivan Alexander conversing familiarly with the various Evangelists, and occupying a place of honour among the souls of the Blessed in the scene of the Last Judgment.

Fig. 19

Plates 48, 50

MUSIC

As the legendary home of Orpheus, Bulgaria is rich in musical tradition. During the period under review, a number of different cultural and ethnic strands united to give this musical tradition a new impetus. The pagan Slavs brought their plaintive chants and the Turkic proto-Bulgars their wild oriental melodies. Following the conversion of Bulgaria in the ninth century, the country echoed to the sound of the Orthodox chant and liturgy, and a corpus of Slavonic hymns grew up, both original and in translation from the Greek.

Musical instruments developed in variety and sophistication. Simple pan-pipes, and stringed instruments of Central Asian type, were supplemented by the flute, the bag-pipes, the cithara and the cymbal, while the Byzantines brought in the pneumatic organ. This wealth of instrumental resources spread all over the Balkans: for example, a fourteenth-century fresco of the Mocking of Christ from Staro Nagorichino in Macedonia depicts two burly fellows blowing long curved trumpets, another banging on a drum suspended round his neck, and a little kneeling figure crashing away at a small pair of cymbals. Again, a scene from Psalm 150 painted on the wall of the monastery church of Lesnovo in Serbia shows a Serbian *kolo* or chain dance, similar to the Bulgarian *khoro*, being performed to the accompaniment of a lute and a drum. Similar scenes can be found on frescoes collected in the Historical

*Fig. 42 John Kukuzel, the eminent
Bulgarian-born reformer of Byzantine music.
From a Psaltery in the library of the Great
Lavra of St Athanasius, on Mount Athos.
Note the boat-shaped hat, characteristic of
Byzantine musicians. (After Naslednikova)*

Museum at Tărnovo. The miniatures in the Bulgarian Manasses chronicle include several examples of cavalrymen startling the enemy with blasts from long thin trumpets with wide mouths.

Other popular instruments were the shawm, a medieval forerunner of the oboe, and the *gusla* or Balkan rebeck, a buzzy, single-stringed horse-hair fiddle, played with a horse-hair bow shaped like a hunting-bow and decorated with a horse's-head pattern.

Plate 62

Though their own musical culture was revolutionized by the impact of Byzantine music, the Bulgarians themselves can claim important achievements in this field. The main contributor to this development appears to have been John Kukuzel or Cucuzeles, who was born at Durazzo (Dyrrachium) in Albania about 1280, though he always considered himself a true Bulgarian.

Fig. 42

When only about ten years old, Kukuzel was sent to Constantinople, to attend the Higher School founded by Emperor Michael VIII Palaeologus to replace the Magnaura academy, which had been closed down by the Crusaders. We are told that he mastered Greek, philosophy, music and calligraphy, and won general commendation. Kukuzel was soon appointed *domestikos* or precentor of the Patriarchal Church and devoted all his free time to composition, rewriting the ancient hymns and devotional odes, such as the *stichera*, *troparia* and *kondakia*; these he embellished beyond recognition, and created his own 'Papadikian' melody on an extended scale. He himself had a remarkably beautiful voice, and was an accomplished interpreter of his own works. Kukuzel soon attracted the attention of Emperor Andronicus II the Old (1282–1328) whose favourite he became.

A number of colourful anecdotes about Kukuzel are included in a fifteenth-century biography of the composer, written by an unknown monk. We gather that in spite of his musical and worldly fame, Kukuzel never forgot his simple Bulgarian family background. This is shown in his original composition, known as 'The Lament of the Bulgarian Woman', the motto of which is his own mother's plaintive cry: 'My beloved child Yovan, where art thou, oh, oh!'

In this context it is worth noting that the very name Kukuzel was originally a nickname given to the composer by his Greek schoolmates, as an allusion to his Bulgarian rustic origins: it means 'broad beans and cabbage'. But so great did his renown become that other composers adopted the name as a form of emulation, so that we find two other fourteenth-century Byzantine musicians styling themselves respectively 'Gregory Kukuzel', and 'Jehoshaphat Kukuzel the Younger'.

In later years, John Kukuzel renounced the world, and spent some time as a humble goat-herd at the Great Lavra of St Athanasius on Mount Athos. He died there at a great age, and was canonized, his feast-day being October 14. Icons representing him are numerous; in most of them he is shown as a tall, handsome man, wearing the boat-shaped hat reserved for eminent Byzantine composers of that period. The revitalizing of Byzantine liturgical music by Kukuzel is certainly one of the most valuable of many contributions made by Bulgaria to the cultural evolution of medieval Christendom.

Bibliography

CHAPTER I

ASSOCIATION INTERNATIONALE D'ÉTUDES DU SUD-EST EUROPÉEN. *Actes du Premier Congrès International des Études Balkaniques et Sud-Est Européennes: III, Histoire* (V^e-XVe ss.; XVe-XVIIe ss.), Sofia 1969.

BIRNBAUM, H. and VRYONIS, S., eds. *Aspects of the Balkans: Continuity and Change*, The Hague 1972.

BULGARIAN ACADEMY OF SCIENCES – Division of Fine Arts and Culture. *Kompleksna nauchna Rodopska ekspeditsiya prez 1953 godina. Dokladi i materiali* (The combined scientific Rhodope expedition of 1953. Reports and materials), Sofia 1955.

— Division of Historical and Pedagogical Sciences. *Narodnostna i bitova obshtnost na Rodopskite Bălgari. Sbornik ot statii* (The national and social community organization of the Rhodope Bulgarians. Collection of articles), Sofia 1969.

— Institute of Balkan Studies. *Recherches de Géographie historique.* Edited by V. Beshev-liev and V. Tăpkova-Zaimova, Sofia 1970.

— Institute of History. *Études Historiques, à l'occasion du 1er Congrès International des Études Balkaniques et Sud-Est Européennes-Sofia,* tom. 3–5, Sofia 1966.

— Institute of History. *Fontes Historiae Bulgaricae.* (*Izvori za bălgarskata istoriya.* Sources on Bulgarian history), tom. 3, etc., Sofia 1958–

— Institute of History. *L'Histoire bulgare dans les ouvrages des Savants européens,* Sofia 1969.

DINEV, L. and MISHEV, K. *Bălgariya. Kratka geografiya* (Bulgaria. A brief geography), Sofia 1969.

EVANS, S. G. *A short History of Bulgaria,* London 1960.

FORBES, N., and others. *The Balkans. A history, etc,* Oxford 1915.

GERASIMOV, I. P., and GĂLĂBOV, ZH. S. *Geografiya na Bălgariya. Părvi tom.: Fizi-cheska geografiya* (Geography of Bulgaria. Vol. 1: Physical geography), Sofia 1966.

HAUSSIG, H. W. *A History of Byzantine Civilization,* London 1971.

HERODOTUS. *The Histories of Herodotus of Halicarnassus,* trans. and introduced by Harry Carter, London 1962.

HODDINOTT, R. F. *Bulgaria in Antiquity,* London 1975.

IVANOV, Y. *Bălgarski starini iz Makedoniya* (Bulgarian antiquities from Macedonia), edited by B. and D. Angelov, Sofia 1970.

KĂNCHOV, V. *Izbrani proizvedeniya* (Selected writings on history, topography, ethno-graphy and geography), edited by Khristo Khristov, 2 vols, Sofia 1970.

KIRKOVA, L. and KOSTOVA-YANKOVA, E. *La Science historique bulgare, 1960–1964. Bibliographie publiée à l'occasion du XIIe Congrès International des Sciences Histor-iques – Vienne, 1965,* Sofia 1965.

MACDERMOTT, M. *A History of Bulgaria, 1393–1885,* London 1962.

The Bulgarians

OBOLENSKY, D. *The Byzantine Common-wealth. Eastern Europe, 500–1453*, London 1971.

TODOROV, N., DINEV, L., and MELNISHKI, L. *Bulgaria. Historical and geographical outline*, Sofia 1968.

TODOROV, N. and others, eds. *Bibliographie d'Études Balkaniques*, vol. 1, etc., Sofia 1968– .

VEYRENC, C. J. *Nagel's Encyclopedia-Guide: Bulgaria*. Geneva 1968. (With excellent notes on leading historical sites and monuments.)

VISHNEVSKI, V., KRĂNZOV, G., and POP-ZLATEV, Z. *Bălgariya i Bălgarinat* (Bulgaria and the Bulgarians), Sofia 1968.

CHAPTER II

ANGELOV, D. 'La formation de la nationalité bulgare', in *Études Balkaniques* (Sofia), 1969, no. 4, pp. 14–37.

— *Obrazuvane na bălgarskata narodnost* (The formation of the Bulgarian nation), Sofia 1971.

ARTAMONOV, M. I. *Istoriya Khazar* (The History of the Khazars), Leningrad 1962. (Russian.)

BESHEVLIEV, V. 'Aus der Geschichte der Protobulgaren', in *Études Balkaniques*, 1970, no. 2, pp. 39–56.

— 'Les cités antiques en Mésie et en Thrace et leur sort à l'époque du Haut Moyen Âge', in *Études Balkaniques*, 1966, no. 5, pp. 207–20.

— 'Deux corrections au "Breviarium" du patriarche Nicephore', in *Revue des Études Byzantines*', tom. XXVIII, 1970, pp. 153–59.

— *Epigrafski prinosi* (Epigraphic contributions), Sofia 1952.

— *Die protobulgarischen Inschriften*, Berlin 1963. (Berliner Byz. Arbeiten, Bd 23.)

— 'Verata na Părvobălgarite' (The religious beliefs of the Proto-Bulgars), in *Annuaire de l'Université de Sofia*, Fac. historico-philologique, XXXV. 1, Sofia 1939.

BESHEVLIEV, V. and IRMSCHER, J., eds. *Antike und Mittelalter in Bulgarien*, Berlin, 1960. (Berliner Byz. Arbeiten, Bd 21.)

BURMOV, A. *Izbrani proizvedeniya v tri toma* (Selected writings, in three volumes). Tom. 1, etc. Sofia, 1968– . (Bulgarian, German and French texts. Vol. 1 contains 22 articles and monographs, including materials on the origins of the Proto-Bulgars.)

DANOV, KHR. 'Social and economic evolution of the Ancient Thracians in Homeric, Archaic and Classical times', in *Études Historiques à l'occasion du XIe Congrès International des Sciences Historiques – Stockholm, 1960*, Sofia 1960, pp. 3–29.

DENISOV, P. V. *Etno-kul'turnye paralleli dunaiskikh Bolgar i Chuvashei* (The ethno-cultural parallels of the Danube Bulgars and the Chuvash), Cheboksary 1969. (Russian.)

DUICHEV (DUJČEV), I. 'Les Slaves et Byzance', in *Études Historiques à l'occasion du XIe Congrès International des Sciences Historiques – Stockholm, août 1960*, Sofia 1960, pp. 31–77.

GIMBUTAS, M. *The Slavs*. (Ancient Peoples and Places), London 1971.

HENSEL, W. *Die Slawen im frühen Mittelalter*, Berlin 1965.

KOLEDAROV, P. S. 'Settlement structure of the Bulgarian Slavs in their transition from a clan to a territorial community', in

Byzantino-Bulgarica, tom. 3, Sofia 1969, pp. 125–32.

MACARTNEY, C. A. Article 'Petchenegs', in *Encyclopaedia Britannica*, 14th edn, vol. 17.

MINORSKY, V., trans. and ed. *Ḥudūd al-'Ālam (The Regions of the World), a Persian Geography, 372 AH–982 AD*. Preface by V. V. Barthold, London 1937.

MORAVCSIK, G. *Byzantinoturcica*. 2 vols, 2nd edn, Berlin 1958.

NÉMETH, J. *La provenance du nom Bulgar*, Winnipeg 1964. (Onomastica, No. 28.)

PRITSAK, O. *Die Bulgarische Fürstenliste und die Sprache der Protobulgaren*, Wiesbaden 1955. (Ural-Altaische Bibliothek, No. 1.)

PROCOPIUS, *Gotenkriege*, edited and translated by Otto Veh, Munich 1966.

ROGEV, B. 'Fondement astronomique de l'ère protobulgare', in *Études Balkaniques*, 1969, no. 3, pp. 72–94.

RYBAKOV, B. A. ed. *Ocherki Istorii SSSR. Krizis rabovladel'cheskoi sistemy i zarozhdenie feodalizma na territorii SSSR, III–IX vv*. (Studies in the History of the USSR. The crisis of the slave owning system and the birth of feudalism on the territory of the USSR, 3rd to 9th centuries AD), Moscow 1958. (Russian.)

TĂPKOVA-ZAIMOVA, V. *Nashestviya i etnicheski promeni na Balkanite prez VI–VII v.* (Invasions et changements ethniques dans les Balkans au VIᵉ–VIIᵉ siècle), Sofia 1966.

— 'Sur les rapports entre la population indigène des régions balkaniques et les "Barbares" au VIᵉ–VIIᵉ siècle', in *Byzantino-Bulgarica*, tom. 1, Sofia 1962, pp. 67–78.

VASMER, M. *Die Slaven in Griechenland*, Berlin 1941.

VENEDIKOV, I. 'Trois inscriptions protobulgares', in *Musée National Bulgare: Fouilles et Recherches*, IV, Sofia 1949, pp. 167–87. (French text, Bulgarian summary.)

CHAPTER III

ADONTZ, N. 'Samuel l'Arménien, roi des Bulgares', in *Études Arméno-Byzantines*, Lisbon 1965, pp. 347–407. (Originally published in *Mémoires publiés par l'Académie royale de Belgique*, Bruxelles 1938.)

ANGELOV, D., GANDEV, KHR., and TODOROV, N., eds. *Istoriya na Bălgariya* (History of Bulgaria, in 3 vols). 2nd edn vol. 1, Sofia 1961.

BESHEVLIEV, V. 'Les inscriptions du relief de Madara', in *Byzantinoslavica*, Prague, vol. 16, 1955, pp. 214–254.

— 'Les inscriptions protobulgares et leur portée culturelle et historique', in *Byzantinoslavica*, Prague, vol. 32/1, 1971, pp. 35–51.

BOZHKOV, A. *Miniatyuri ot Madridskiya răkopis na Ioan Skilitsa* (Miniatures from the Madrid manuscript of John Scylitzes), Sofia 1972.

BROWNING, R. *Byzantium and Bulgaria*. London, Berkeley, and Los Angeles 1975.

BULGARIAN ACADEMY OF SCIENCES – Institute of History. *Byzantino-Bulgarica*, tom. 1–3, etc., Sofia 1962– .

DIMITROV, D. I. 'Rannebolgarskie nekropoli v Varnenskom raione' (Early Bulgar cemeteries in the Varna region), in *Mezhdunarodny Simpozium Slavyanskoi Arkheologii, 21–28 IV 1970 g*. (International Symposium of Slavonic Archaeology, 21–28 April 1970), Sofia 1970. (Russian.)

DZHAMBOV, K. *Arkheologicheski otkritiya za istoriyata na Plovdiv i Plovdivskiya krai* (Archaeological discoveries on the history of Plovdiv and the Plovdiv region), Plovdiv 1964.

— 'Prinos kăm prouchvane na slavyanskata keramika v Plovdivskiya krai' (Contribution to the study of Slavonic pottery in the Plovdiv region), in *GNAMP* (Annual of the Plovdiv Archaeological Museum), IV, 1960.

DZHINGOV, G. 'Gorodishche epokhi rannego srednevekov'ya u s. Styrmen v Bolgarii' (The ruined town from the early medieval period close to the village of Styrmen in Bulgaria), in *Sovetskaya Arkheologiya* (Soviet Archaeology), Moscow 1968, No. 2, pp. 277–88. (Russian.)

GYUZELEV, V. *Knyaz Boris părvi. Bălgariya prez vtorata polovina na IX vek* (Prince Boris I. Bulgaria during the second half of the ninth century), Sofia 1969.

HUSSEY, J. M., ed. *The Cambridge Medieval History*. 2nd edn, vol. IV: *The Byzantine Empire*. parts 1 and 2, Cambridge, 1966–67. (See especially Chap. XI, 'The Empire and its Northern Neighbours, 565–1018' by D. Obolensky, with specialized bibliography and list of rulers.)

KOSEV, D., KHRISTOV, KH., and ANGELOV, D. *Kratka Istoriya na Bălgariya* (Brief history of Bulgaria). 2nd edn, Sofia 1969. (Useful also for other sections of the present work.)

LISHEV, S. *Za pronikvaneto i rolyata na parite văv feodalna Bălgariya* (On the penetration

and the role of coined money in feudal Bulgaria), Sofia 1958.

— *Za stokovoto proizvodstvo văv feodalna Bălgariya* (Production of marketable goods in feudal Bulgaria), Sofia 1957.

OSTROGORSKY, G. *History of the Byzantine State*, trans. by Joan Hussey. 2nd edn, Oxford 1968.

PAISIY HILENDARSKI. (Monk Paisi of Hilendar Monastery). *Slavyano-Bălgarska istoriya* (The Slavo-Bulgarian history), edited by P. Dinekov, Sofia 1972.

PRIMOV, B. 'Certain aspects of the international importance of the First Bulgarian Empire', in *Études Historiques à l'occasion du XIII Congrès International des Sciences Historiques – Moscou, août 1970,* tom. V, Sofia 1970, pp. 191–217.

RUNCIMAN, S. *A History of the First Bulgarian Empire*, London 1930.

SERGHERAERT, G. (Christian Gérard). *Les Bulgares de la Volga et les Slaves du Danube*, Paris 1939.

— *Syméon le Grand (893–927),* Paris 1960.

STANCHEV, S., and others. *Nadpisăt na Chărgubilya Mostich* (The inscription of Chărgubilya Mostich), Sofia 1955.

TĂPKOVA-ZAIMOVA, V. 'L'idée byzantine de l'unité du monde et l'état bulgare', in *Association Internationale d'Études du Sud-Est Européen: Actes du Premier Congrès International des Études Balkaniques et Sud-Est Européennes,* III, Sofia 1969, pp. 291–298.

TOYNBEE, A. *Constantine Porphyrogenitus and his world.* Oxford 1973.

TZENOFF, G. *Geschichte der Bulgaren und der anderen Südslaven von der römischen Eroberung der Balkanhalbinsel an bis zum Ende des neunten Jahrhunderts,* Berlin and Leipzig 1935.

VĂZHAROVA, Z. *Slavyano-Bălgarskoto selishte krai selo Popina, Silistrensko* (The Slavo-Bulgarian settlement near the village of Popina in the Silistra Region), Sofia 1956.

— *Slavyanski i slavyanobalgarski selishta v bălgarskite zemi ot kraya na VI.–XI. vek* (Slavonic and Slavo-Bulgarian settle-ments on Bulgarian territory from the end of the 6th up to the 11th century), Sofia 1965.

ZAIMOV, Y. *Bitolski nadpis na Ivan Vladislav, Samodărzhets Bălgarski, etc.* (The Bitolja inscription of Ivan Vladislav, the Bul-garian Autocrat. An Old Bulgarian monument, 1015/1016), Sofia 1970.

ZLATARSKI, V. N. *Istoriya na Bălgarskata dărzhava prez srednite vekove,* tom. 1: *Părvo Bălgarsko tsarstvo* (History of the Bulgarian State in the Middle Ages, vol. 1: The First Bulgarian Empire). Pt 1, 2, Sofia 1918, 1927. (Later reprinted, various dates.)

CHAPTER IV

ANDREEV, M., and ANGELOV, D. *Istoriya na bălgarskata feodalna dărzhava i pravo* (His-tory of the Bulgarian feudal state and legal system), 4th edn, Sofia 1972.

ANGELOV, D. 'Die bulgarischen Länder and das bulgarische Volk in den Grenzen des byzantinischen Reiches im XI.–XII. Jahrhundert (1018–1185)', in *Proceedings of the XIIIth International Congress of Byzantine Studies, Oxford, 5–10 September 1966,* London 1967, pp. 151–75.

BULGARIAN ACADEMY OF SCIENCES – Institute of History. *Documents and*

Materials on the history of the Bulgarian People, Sofia 1969.

CARTER, F. W. *Dubrovnik (Ragusa): a classic city state,* London and New York 1972. (See especially the chapter entitled 'Balkan trade through Dubrovnik, 1358–1500'.)

DUICHEV (DUJČEV), I. *Bălgarsko srednove-kovie, etc.* (Studies in the political and cultural history of medieval Bulgaria), Sofia 1972.

GORINA, L. V. *Sotsial'no-ekonomicheskie otno-sheniya vo vtorom bolgarskom tsartve* (Social and economic relationships under the Second Bulgarian Empire), Moscow 1972. (Russian.)

HEYD, W. *Histoire du Commerce du Levant au Moyen-Age,* édition française . . . par Furcy Raynaud, 2 vols, Leipzig 1885–86: reprinted Amsterdam 1959.

HUSSEY, J. M. ed. *The Cambridge Medieval History.* 2nd edn, vol. IV: *The Byzantine Empire,* parts 1 and 2, Cambridge, 1966–67. (See especially chap. XII, 'The Balkans, 1018–1499', by M. Dinić, with specialized bibliography and list of rulers.)

IL'INSKY, G. A. *Gramoty bolgarskikh carey.* (Charters of the Bulgarian tsars), re-printed with introduction by Ivan Dujčev, London 1970.

KOLEDAROV, P. S. 'Nai-ranni spomen-avaniya na Bălgarite vărkhu starinnite karti' (The earliest references to the Bul-garians on ancient maps), in *Izvestiya* (Bulletin) of the Historical Institute of the Bulgarian Academy of Sciences, tom. 20, 1968, pp. 219–54.

LISHEV, S. *Bălgarskiyat srednevekoven grad. Obshtestveno-ikonomicheski oblik* (The Bul-

garian medieval town. Social and economic outline), Sofia 1970.

LITAVRIN, G. G. *Bolgariya i Vizantiya v XI–
XII v.* (Bulgaria and Byzantium in the
11th–12th centuries), Moscow 1960.
(Russian.)

METCALF, D. M. *Coinage in the Balkans,
820–1355,* Thessaloniki 1965.

MUSHMOV, N. A. *Monetite i pechatite na
bălgarskite tsare. Numismatique et sigillo-
graphie bulgares,* Sofia 1924.

MUTAFCHIEV, P. *Istoriya na bălgarski narod.*
(History of the Bulgarian people). 2nd
edn, edited by Ivan Duichev, 2 vols,
Sofia 1943–44.

—*Izbrani proizvedeniya v dva toma* (Selected
historical writings, in 2 vols), edited by
D. Angelov, Sofia 1973.

MUTAFCHIEVA, V. *Poslednite Shishmanovtsi*
(The last of the Shishman dynasty), Sofia
1969.

NIKOV, P. *Bălgaro-ungarski otnosheniya ot
1257 do 1277 godina* (Bulgarian-
Hungarian relations from 1257 to 1277),
Sofia 1919. (Offprint from Bk 11 of the
Sbornik of the Bulgarian Academy of
Sciences.)

PRIMOV, B. 'The Papacy, the Fourth
Crusade and Bulgaria', in *Byzantino-
Bulgarica,* tom. I, 1962, pp. 183–211.

SETTON, K. M., general ed. *A History of the
Crusades.* Vol. II, Philadelphia 1962.

SKAZKIN, S. D., chief ed. *Istoriya Vizantii v
trekh tomakh* (History of Byzantium, in 3
vols), Moscow 1967. (Russian.)

SWEENEY, J. R. 'Basil of Trnovo's Journey
to Durazzo', in *Slavonic and East European
Review,* vol. LI, no. 122, January 1973,
pp. 118–23.

TSANKOVA-PETKOVA, G. *Za agrarnite otno-*

*sheniya v srednovekovna Bălgariya (XI–
XIII v.) – Sur les rapports agraires en
Bulgarie au Moyen Age (XI–XIIIe S.),*
Sofia 1964.

WOLFF, R. L. 'The "Second Bulgarian
Empire". Its origin and history to 1204',
in *Speculum,* (Cambridge, Mass.), Vol.
XXIV, April, 1949, No. 2, pp. 167–206.

ZLATARSKI, V. N. *Istoriya na Bălgarskata
dărzhava prez srednite vekove,* tom. 2:
Bălgariya pod vizantiysko vladichestvo (1018–
1187) (History of the Bulgarian State in
the Middle Ages, vol. 2: Bulgaria under
Byzantine domination, 1018–1187), Sofia
1934.

— tom. 3: *Vtoro Bălgarska tsarstvo: Bălgariya
pri Asenevtsi (1187–1280)* (The Second
Bulgarian Empire: Bulgaria under the
Assen dynasty, 1187–1280), Sofia 1940.
(Both later reprinted, various dates.)

—*Izbrani proizvedeniya v cheteri toma* (Selected
historical writings in 4 vols), edited by
Petăr Petrov, vol. 1, etc., Sofia 1972– .

— *Sbornik v chest na Vasil N. Zlatarski*
(Festschrift in honour of V. N. Zlatarski:
Essays on Bulgarian history, by his
colleagues and pupils), Sofia 1925.

CHAPTER V

ANGELOV, D. *Bogomilstvoto v Bălgariya*
(Bogomilism in Bulgaria), Sofia 1969.

— 'Le mouvement bogomile dans les pays
balkaniques et son influence en Europe
occidentale', in *Actes du Colloque International de Civilisations Balkaniques, Sinaïa,*
juillet 1962, pp. 173–82.

— 'Rationalistic Ideas of a Medieval Heresy',
in: Georgiev, E. and others, *Bulgaria's
Share in Human Culture,* Sofia 1968, pp.
55–86.

Bibliography

ANGELOV, D., PRIMOV, B., and BATAKLIEV, G. *Bogomilstvoto v Bălgariya, Vizantiya i Zapadna Evropa v izvori* (Bogomilism in Bulgaria, Byzantium and Western Europe in original sources), Sofia 1967.

BEGUNOV, Y. K. *Kozma Presviter v slavyanskikh literaturakh* (Cosmas the Priest in the Slavonic literatures), Sofia 1973. (Russian.)

BIHALJI-MERIN, O. and BENAC, A. *The Bogomils,* London 1964.

COMNENA, PRINCESS ANNA. *The Alexiad.* Trans. Elizabeth A. S. Dawes, London 1928; reprinted 1967.

GARSOÏAN, N. G. *The Paulician Heresy,* The Hague and Paris 1967.

IVANOV, Y. *Bogomilski knigi i legendi* (Bogomil books and legends), Sofia 1925, reprinted 1970.

OBOLENSKY, D. *The Bogomils, A Study in Balkan neo-Manichaeism,* Cambridge 1948.

PRIMOV, B. *Bugrite. Kniga za pop Bogomil i negovite Posledovateli* (The Bougres. A book about Priest Bogomil and his followers), Sofia 1970.

— 'Medieval Bulgaria and the Dualistic Heresies in Western Europe', in *Études Historiques à l'occasion du XIᵉ Congrès International des Sciences Historiques – Stockholm, août 1960,* Sofia 1960, pp. 79–106.

PUECH, H. C. and VAILLANT, A. *Le Traité contre les Bogomiles de Cosmas le Prêtre,* Paris 1945.

RUNCIMAN, S. *The Medieval Manichee: A Study of the Christian Dualist Heresy,* Cambridge 1947, reprinted 1955, 1960.

TOPENTCHAROV, V. *Bou (l) gres et Cathares: Deux brasiers – une même flamme,* Paris 1971.

ZAITSEV, V. K. *Bogomilskoe dvizhenie i obshchestvennaya zhizn' Severnoi Italii epokhi duchento* (The Bogomil movement and social life in Northern Italy in the 12th century), Minsk 1967. (Russian.)

CHAPTER VI

ANGELOV, B. ST. *Iz starata bălgarska, ruska i srăbska literatura* (Studies in Old Bulgarian, Russian and Serbian literature), bk 2, Sofia 1967.

BDINSKI ZBORNIK. *Old Slavonic menologium, AD 1360.* Facsimile edition, Codex Gandavensis 408, with a presentation by Ivan Dujčev. London 1972.

BOGDANOV, I. *Patriarkh Evtimy* (Patriarch Euthymius), Sofia 1971.

BULGARIAN ACADEMY OF SCIENCES. *Tărnovska knizhovna shkola, 1371–1971. Mezhdunaroden simposium.* (The Tărnovo literary school, 1371–1971. An international symposium), Sofia 1974.

CLEMENT OF OHRIDA, SAINT. *Grătskite zhitiya na Kliment Ohridski* (The Greek biographies of Clement of Ohrida), edited by A. Milev, Sofia 1966.

— *Kliment Okhridski. Materiali za negovoto chestvuvane po sluchai 1050 godini ot smărtta mu* (Clement of Ohrida. Materials to commemorate the 1050th anniversary of his death). Bulgarian Academy of Sciences: Sofia 1968.

— *Kliment Okhridski. Sbornik ot statii po sluchai 1050 godini ot smărtta mu* (Clement of Ohrida. Collection of articles on the occasion of the 1050th anniversary of his death), Sofia 1966.

— *Săbrani săchineniya* (Collected writings, critical edition), edited by B. St. Angelov, K. M. Kuev and Khr. Kodov, vol. I, etc. Sofia 1970 – (in progress).

CONSTANTINE MANASSES. *Letopista na*

The Bulgarians

Konstantin Manasi (Chronicle or 'Historical Synopsis'), facsimile edition of the illuminated Vatican manuscript of the Slavonic version, edited by Ivan Duichev, Sofia 1963.

CYRIL AND METHODIUS, SAINTS. *Konstantin-Kiril Filosof. Yubileen sbornik po sluchai 1100-godishninata ot smårtta mu* (Constantine-Cyril the Philosopher. A jubilee symposium on the occasion of the 1100th anniversary of his death). Issued by the Institute of Literature of the Bulgarian Academy of Sciences, Sofia 1969.

— *L'Oeuvre de Constantin-Cyrille le Philosophe: Monographies.* Sofia, n.d. (about 1969).

DANCHEV, G. *Vladislav Gramatik: Knizhovnik i pisatel* (Vladislav the Grammarian. A study of the 15th-century Bulgarian scribe and author), Sofia 1969.

DINEKOV, P., chief ed. *Istoriya na bålgarskata literatura. tom. 1: Starobålgarskata literatura* (History of Bulgarian literature. Vol. 1: Old Bulgarian literature), Sofia 1963.

— *Starobålgarski stranitsi. Antologiya* (Pages of Old Bulgarian literature, an anthology), Sofia 1966.

DRAGOVA, N. *Kliment Okhridski* (St Clement of Ohrida), Sofia 1966.

DUJČEV (DUICHEV), I. *Slavia Orthodoxa: collected studies in the history of the Slavic Middle Ages,* reprinted, London 1972.

— ed. *Bononski Psaltir. Bålgarski knizhoven pametnik ot XIII vek* (Psalterium Bononiense. A Bulgarian literary monument of the 13th century), Sofia 1968.

DVORNIK, F. *Byzantine missions among the Slavs,* Rutgers University Press, New Brunswick, New Jersey 1970.

EUTHYMIUS, PATRIARCH OF BULGARIA. *Werke des Patriarchen von Bulgarien Euthymius (1375–1393), nach den besten Handschriften herausgegeben von Emil Kałužniacki,* Vienna 1901; reprinted, with introduction by Ivan Dujčev, London 1971.

GEORGIEV, E., ed. *"Pokhvalno slovo za Evtimy" ot Grigory Tsamblak* (The Eulogy of Patriarch Euthymius, by Gregory Tsamblak), Sofia 1972.

GOSHEV, I. *Rilski glagolicheski listove.* (The Rila glagolitic folios), Sofia 1956.

— *Starobålgarski glagolicheski i kirilski nadpisi ot IX i X v.* (Old Bulgarian Glagolitic and Cyrillic inscriptions from the 9th and 10th centuries), Sofia 1961.

IL'INSKY, G. A. *Opyt sistematicheskoi Kirillo-Mefod'evskoi bibliografii* (Attempt at a systematic bibliography of Saints Cyril and Methodius), Sofia 1934. (Russian.)

IVANOVA, A. *Troyanski Damaskin. Bålgarski pametnik ot XVII vek* (The Troyan codex of the writings of Damaskenos Studites. A Bulgarian monument of the 17th century), Sofia 1967.

IVANOVA-KONSTANTINOVA, K. 'Pålen tekst na Slovoto za Sretenie ot Ioan Ekzarkh' (The complete text of the Homily on Candlemas by John the Exarch), in *Izvestiya* (Bulletin) of the Institute of Bulgarian Language of the Bulgarian Academy of Sciences, bk 20, Sofia 1971, pp. 239–62.

JOHN THE EXARCH (Ioan Ekzarkh Bålgarski). *Slova* (Homilies), edited by Dora Ivanova-Mircheva. tom. 1, etc. Sofia 1971– .

KALUŽNIACKI, E. *Aus der panegyrischen Litteratur der Südslaven.* Vienna, 1901, reprinted London 1971.

KAWERAU, P. *Das Christentum des Ostens,* Stuttgart 1972.

KODOV, KHR. *Opis na slavyanskite răkopisi v Bibliotekata na Bălgarskata Akademiya na Naukite* (Description of the Slavonic manuscripts in the library of the Bulgarian Academy of Sciences), Sofia 1970.

KUEV, K. M. *Chernorizets Khrabăr* (A study of the Old Bulgarian writer), Sofia 1967.

KUSSEFF, M. Article, 'Old Bulgarian Literature', in *The Penguin Companion to Literature,* vol. 2, Harmondsworth, 1969, pp. 577–81, with bibliography.

MEYENDORFF, J. *Byzantine Hesychasm: historical, theological and social problems,* London 1974.

MIRCHEV, K., and KODOV, KHR. *Eninski Apostol. Starobălgarski pametnik ot XI vek* (The Codex Eninensis, or Enina Praxapostolus, an Old Bulgarian monument of the 11th century), Sofia 1965.

MOSER, C. A. *A History of Bulgarian Literature, 865–1944.* The Hague and Paris 1972.

OBOLENSKY, D. *Byzantium and the Slavs: collected studies,* London 1971.

PANDURSKI, V., and BOSSILKOV, S. *Cyril and Methodius in Rome,* Sofia 1970.

PETKANOVA/TOTEVA, D. *Damaskinite v bălgarskata literatura* (The writings of Damaskenos Studites in Bulgarian literature), Sofia 1965.

RUSEV, P., and DAVIDOV, A. *Grigory Tsamblak v Rumăniya i v starata rumănska literatura* (Gregory Tsamblak in Romania and in ancient Romanian literature), Sofia 1966.

SIMEON LOGOTHETES. *Slavyansky perevod khroniki Simeona Logotheta* (The Slavonic translation of the chronicle of Simeon Logothetes). Edited by V. I. Sreznevsky, St Petersburg, 1905, and reprinted with studies by G. Ostrogorsky and Ivan Duichev, London 1971.

SYRKU, P. A. *K istorii ispravlenii knig v Bolgarii v XIV veke* (On the history of book revision in Bulgaria in the 14th century), 2 vols, St Petersburg, 1890–98; reprinted, with introd. by Ivan Duichev, London 1972. (Russian.)

CHAPTER VII

Architecture

ANCHEV, A., and others. *National Museum: Rila Monastery,* Sofia 1965.

ANTONOVA, V. *Madara. Istoriko-arkheologicheski rezervat* (Madara. Guide to the historical and archaeological protected area), Sofia 1970.

— *Pliska: Vodach* (Guide to Pliska). 3rd edn, Sofia 1967.

—and others. *Muzei i pametnitsi na kulturata v Shumen i Shumenski okrăg. Pătevoditel* (Museums and cultural monuments in Shumen and the Shumen district. A guide), Sofia 1970.

ATANASOVA, Y., GEORGIEV, N., and MIKHAILOV, P. *Vidin,* Sofia 1968.

BICHEV, M. *Architecture in Bulgaria, from ancient times to the late 19th century,* Sofia 1961.

BOGDANOV, I. *Veliko Turnovo,* Sofia 1967.

BOYADZHIEV, ST. 'L'ancienne église metropole de Nesebăr', in *Byzantino-Bulgarica,* tom. 1, Sofia 1962, pp. 321–46.

— 'L'église du village Vinica à la lumière de nouvelles données', in *Byzantino-Bulgarica,* tom. 2, Sofia 1966, pp. 241–65.

BRENTJES, B. 'On the Prototype of the

Proto-Bulgarian Temples at Pliska, Preslav and Madara', in *East and West* (Rome), New series, vol. 21, nos 3–4, Sept.–Dec. 1971, pp. 213–16.

BULGARIAN ACADEMY OF SCIENCES – Archaeological Institute and Museum. *Nessèbre,* premier volume, etc. Auteurs, Iv. Venedikov, etc., Sofia 1969– .

— *Tsarevgrad Tărnov. Dvoretsat na Bălgar-skite Tsare prez vtorata bălgarska dărzhava* (The royal city of Tărnovo. The palace of the Bulgarian tsars during the Second Bulgarian Empire). tom. 1, etc., Sofia 1973– .

CHAVRĂKOV, G. I. *Bălgarski manastiri* (Bulgarian monasteries). Sofia 1974.

CHOKOISKA, V. *Ukazatel za pametnitsite na kulturata v Asenovgrad i blizkata okolnost* (Guide to the cultural monuments at Assenovgrad and its neighbourhood). Assenovgrad, (*about* 1960).

DIMITROV, D. P., and others. *Kratkaya istoriya bolgarskoi arkhitektury* (Brief history of Bulgarian architecture), Sofia 1969. (Russian: original Bulgarian version published 1965.)

DZHAMBOV, K. 'Srednevekovna tsărkva i nekropol pri s. Khvoina' (Medieval church and burial ground near the village of Khvoina), in *GNAMP* (Annual of the Plovdiv Archaeological Museum), 1968.

FILOW, B. D. *L'Ancien Art Bulgare,* Berne 1919.

GĂLĂBOV, I. *Nesebăr i negovite pametnitsi* (Nessebăr and its architectural monuments). 2nd edn., Sofia 1961.

GERASIMOV, T., ed. *Serdika. Arkheologicheski materiali i prouchvaniya* (Serdica.

Archaeological materials and studies). tom. 1, etc., Sofia 1964– .

GRABAR, A. *Byzantium : Byzantine art in the Middle Ages,* trans. by Betty Forster, London 1966.

HODDINOTT, R. F. *Early Byzantine Churches in Macedonia and Southern Serbia,* London 1963.

— 'Zapadni vliyaniya vărkhu Krăglata tsărkva v Preslav – Influences occidentales dans l'Eglise Ronde de Preslav', in *Arkheologiya* (Sofia) X, 1, 1968, pp. 20–32.

IVANCHEV, I. *Nesebăr i negovite kăshti* (Nessebăr and its houses), Sofia 1957.

IVANOVA-MAVRODINOVA, V. *Preslav. Vodach za starinite i muzeya* (Preslav. Guide to the Antiquities and the Museum), 2nd edn, Sofia 1966.

KARANESHEV, N. K. *Istoriya na Obshtezhitelniya Monastir "Sv. Preobrazhenie Gospodne" pri V. Tărnovo* (History of the Preobrazhenski Monastery near Great Tărnovo), Great Tărnovo 1927.

KLIMENT RILETS, Archimandrite *Bachkovski Manastir. Kratăk pătevoditel* (The Bachkovo monastery: A brief guide), Sofia 1967.

— *Sv. Ivan Rilski i Rilskiyat Manastir* (St John of Rila and the Rila Monastery), Sofia 1947.

KOSTOVA, A., and KOSTOV, K. *Bachkovski Manastir* (The Bachkovo Monastery), Sofia 1963.

MAVRODINOV, N. *Boyanskata tsărkva i neinite stenopisi.* (The Boyana church and its mural paintings), Sofia 1943.

— *Ednokorabnata i krăstovidna tsărkva po bălgarskite zemi do kraya na XIV v.* (Single nave and cruciform churches in the

Bulgarian lands until the end of the 14th century), Sofia 1931.

MIYATEV (MIATEV), KR. *Arkhitekturata v srednovekovna Bălgariya* (Architecture in medieval Bulgaria), Sofia 1965.

NIKOLOVA, Y., DRAGANOVA, T., and NURKOV, K. *Veliko Tărnovo. Pătevoditel* (Great Tărnovo. A guide), Sofia 1965.

PROTIĆ, A. *Arkhitektonicheskata forma na Sofiyskata tsărkva Sv. Sofiya. Khudoz-hestveno-istorichesko izsledvane* (The archi-tectonic form of the church of St Sophia at Sofia. An artistic and historical study), Sofia 1912.

SHANIDZE, A. *Gruzinsky monastyr' v Bolgarii i ego Tipik* (The Georgian monastery in Bulgaria and its Typicon), Tbilisi 1971. (Georgian and Russian.)
— *Veliky Domestik Zapada Grigory Bakuri-anis-dze i gruzinsky monastyr', osnovanny im v Bolgarii* (The Grand Domesticos of the West, Gregory Bakurianis-dze and the Georgian monastery founded by him in Bulgaria), Tbilisi 1970. (Russian.)

STANCHEV-VAKLINOV, ST., ed. *Preslav: Sbornik* (Preslav: Symposium of articles, sponsored by the Preslav Archaeological Society, 'Ticha'). tom. I, *etc.*, Sofia 1968- .

STOIKOV, G. *Arkhitekturni problemi na Boyan-skata tsărkva* (Architectural problems of the Boyana church), Sofia 1965.
— *Boyana Church*, Sofia 1954. (Studies in Bulgaria's Architectural Heritage, vol. 4.)

TOTEV, T. *Arkheologicheski Muzei, Preslav* (The Preslav Archaeological Museum), Sofia 1969. (French version also avail-able.)

VASILIEV, A. *Troyanski Manastir* (The Troyan Monastery), Sofia 1962.

Painting and Manuscript Illumination

AKRABOVA-ŽANDOVA, I. *Ikoni v Sofiyskiya arkheologicheski Muzei. Datirani ikoni* (Icons in the Sofia Archaeological Museum: dated icons), Sofia 1965.

BAKALOVA, E. *Murals in the Bachkovo ossuary.* (Text with 24 coloured slides), Sofia 1967.

BICHEV, M. *Stenopisite v Ivanovo* (Fresco paintings at Ivanovo), Sofia 1965.

BOSSILKOV, S. *12 Icons of Bulgaria.* 2nd edn, Sofia 1968.

BOZHKOV, A. *Bălgarskata istoricheska zhivopis: Miniatyuri, ikoni, stenopisi* (Bulgarian his-torical painting: Miniatures, icons and fresco paintings), Sofia 1974.
— *Bulgarian Art,* Sofia 1964.
— *Die bulgarische Malerei,* Recklinghausen 1969.

BOZHKOV, A., and CHERNEV, C. *Nationale Kunstgalerie, Sofia: Antike und mittelalter-liche Kunst,* Sofia 1967.

CHERNEV, C. *Narodny stil' v drevnebolgarskoi zhivopisi* (The popular style in Old Bulgarian painting), Sofia 1969. (Rus-sian; also English version: *Popular style in Old Bulgarian art.*)

DER NERSESSIAN, S. 'Two Slavonic paral-lels of the Greek Tetraevangelion: Paris 74', in Der Nersessian, S., *Études Byzantines et Arméniennes,* Louvain 1973, tom. I, pp. 231–63; tom. 2, plates 39–59.

DIMITROV, Z., and SHAROV, B. *Mural ornaments from south-west Bulgaria,* Sofia 1965.

DUJČEV (DUICHEV), I. *Die Miniaturen der Manasses-Chronik.* Sofia and Leipzig 1965.

FILOW, B. D. 'Londonskoto Evangelie na Ivan Aleksandra i negovite minia-tyuri' (The London Gospel manuscript

The Bulgarians

of Tsar Ivan Alexander and its minia-
tures), in *Spisanie* (Review) of the Bul-
garian Academy of Sciences, Bk
XXXVIII, Sofia 1928, pp. 1–32, plates
I–VI.
— *Les Miniatures de l'Évangile du roi Jean
Alexandre à Londres*, Sofia 1934. (Monu-
menta Artis Bulgariae, vol. 3.)
GRABAR, A. *Bulgarian mediaeval wall paintings.*
Introduction by Krsto Mijatev, New
York 1961.
— *La Peinture religieuse en Bulgarie*, 2 vols,
Paris 1928.
KRĂSTEV, K. *Nachenki na Renesans v sred-
novekovna Bălgariya* (Renaissance elements
in medieval Bulgaria). Sofia 1971.
KRĂSTEV, K., and ZAKHARIEV, V. *Stara
bălgarska zhivopis* (Old Bulgarian paint-
ing), Sofia 1960.
L'VOVA, E. *Iskusstvo Bolgarii: Ocherki*
(Studies on Bulgarian art), Moscow
1971. (Russian.)
MAVRODINOV, N. *Rospisi boyanskoi tserkvi*
(The mural paintings of Boyana church),
Sofia 1946. (Russian.)
— *Starobălgarskoto izkustvo. Izkustvoto na păr-
voto bălgarsko tsarstvo* (Old Bulgarian art.
Art of the First Bulgarian Empire), Sofia
1959.
— *Starobălgarskoto izkustvo, XI–XIII v.* (Old
Bulgarian art, of the 11th to the 13th
century), Sofia 1966.
PANAYOTOVA, D. *The Boyana Murals.* (Text
with 24 coloured slides), Sofia 1966.
— *Bulgarian mural paintings of the 14th century,*
Sofia 1966.
STOYANOV, M. *Ukrasa na bălgarskite răkopisi.*
(The ornamentation of Bulgarian manu-
scripts), Sofia 1971.
— *Ukrasa na slavyanskite răkopisi v Bălgariya*

(The ornamentation of Slavonic manu-
scripts in Bulgaria), Sofia 1973.
TALBOT RICE, D. *Byzantine Art.* New edn,
Harmondsworth 1968.
— *Byzantine Painting: the last phase,* London
1968.
TSANOVA, G., and GETOV, L. *Trakiiskata
grobnitsa pri Kazanlăk* (The Thracian
tomb at Kazanluk), Sofia 1970.
VASILIEV, A. *Ivanovskite stenopisi* (The fres-
coes of Ivanovo), Sofia 1953.
— *Sotsialni i patriotichni temi v staroto bălgarsko
izkustvo* (Social and patriotic themes in
Old Bulgarian art), Sofia 1973.
VELMANS, T. 'Les Fresques d'Ivanovo et la
peinture byzantine à la fin du Moyen
Age', in *Journal des Savants,* January–
March 1965, pp. 358–404, plates I–VIII.
WALTER, C. 'Lazarus a Bishop', in *Revue
des Études Byzantines,* vol. XXVII, Paris
1969, pp. 197–208.
WEITZMANN, K., CHATZIDAKIS, M.,
MIATEV, KR. and RADOJČIĆ, S. *Icons
from South Eastern Europe and Sinai,*
London 1968.

Applied Arts

BUYUKLIEV, K., and others. *Musée National
Stara Zagora, Art ancien,* Sofia 1965.
DIMITROV, D. I., and others. *Archäolo-
gisches Museum Varna,* Sofia 1965.
DRUMEV, D., and VASILIEV, A. *Wood-
carving in Bulgaria,* Sofia 1955.
DZHAMBOV, K. 'Novi danni za vodosnab-
dyavaneto na Plovdiv prez antichnostta i
srednovekovieto' (New data on the water
supply of Plovdiv in Antiquity and in the
Middle Ages), in *GNAMP* (Annual
of the Plovdiv Archaeological Museum),
1968.

GOROV, G. and others. *Musée Archéologique de Bourgas: filiales à Nessèbre et Sozopol,* Sofia 1967.

MAVRODINOV, N. *Le Trésor protobulgare de Nagyszentmiklós,* Budapest 1943.

MIYATEV, KR. *Preslavskata keramika* (The ceramic art of Preslav), Sofia 1936.

NASLEDNIKOVA, V. *Istoriya na bǎlgarskiya kostium* (History of Bulgarian costume), Sofia 1969.

VǍRBANOVA, M., ed. *Museen und Kulturden-kmäler im Kreis Burgas,* Sofia 1971.

VASILIEV, A. *Kamenni relefi* (Stone bas-reliefs), Sofia 1959.

VELIKO TǍRNOVO. District Museum of Great Tǎrnovo. *Izvestia* (Bulletin). *Mitteilungen des Bezirksmuseums Tirnovo.* Bk 1, etc., Varna 1962– .

Music

DJOUDJEFF, S. *Rythme et mesure dans la musique populaire bulgare,* Paris 1931.

GOSHEV, I. *Starobǎlgarskata liturgiya* (The Old Bulgarian liturgy, Sofia 1932. (Re-

printed from the *Godishnik* or Annual of Sofia University.)

PALIKAROVA-VERDEIL, R. *La Musique byzantine chez les Bulgares et les Russes (du IXe au XIVe siècle),* Copenhagen 1953.

PETROV, S., and KODOV, K. *Starobǎlgarski muzikalni pametnitsi* (Old Bulgarian musical documents), Sofia 1973.

TODOROVA, Z. 'Yoan Koukouzel – A Medieval Composer', in Georgiev, E. and others, *Bulgaria's Share in Human Culture,* Sofia 1968, pp. 113–30.

VELIMIROVIĆ, M. 'The Influence of the Byzantine Chant on the Music of the Slavic Countries', in *Proceedings of the XIIIth International Congress of Byzantine Studies, Oxford, 5–10 September 1966,* London 1967, pp. 119–40. (Followed by: Supplementary paper by Dimitrije Stefanović, pp. 141–47).

VERKOVIĆ, S. *Narodni pesni na makedonskite Bǎlgari* (Popular songs of the Macedonian Bulgarians). Bk 1, etc., Sofia 1966– .

WELLESZ, E. *Eastern Elements in Western Chant,* Oxford and Boston 1947.

Sources of Illustrations

The majority of the plates, and many of the line drawings, are reproduced from photographs and from field reports kindly supplied at various times by the Bulgarian Committee for Friendship and Cultural Relations with Foreign Countries, Dondukov Boulevard, Sofia. Grateful acknow/ledgment is accorded to this generous and helpful body. In addition, warm thanks are extended to the undermentioned persons and insti/tutions for individual photographs (numerals refer to the plate numbers).

Barber Institute of Fine Art, University of Birmingham, courtesy of the Director and Mr Timothy J. Boatswain: 55; the Trustees of the British Library: 48, 50; Courtauld Institute of Art, University of London, and Dr Robin Cormack: 29–32; Karadimchev Studio, Sofia, courtesy Mrs Elka Bakalova: 35; Kunsthistorisches Museum, Vienna: 12–16; Mrs Mercia MacDermott: 61, 62; Monastery Museum, Rila: 46, 51; National Archaeological Museum, Sofia: 37, 38, 47; Preslav Museum: 18, 22, 45; Regional Historical Museum, Great Tărnovo, courtesy Dr Khristo Nurkov: 52–54, 56; Varna Archaeo/logical Museum and Mr Alexander Kuzov: 9–11, 33, 34.

1

2

3

4

5

6

7

8

9

10

11

12

13

14

15

16

17

18

19

20

21

22

23

24

26

Стый іѡанъ рыльскый
Стый іѡанъ Бгословъ

ІИС ХС

Изобразыса сіа ікона при всечестномъ отцѣ нашемъ ігуменѣ Кірѣ Герасымѣ
Иждывеніемъ же Боголюбывыхъ Ктыторей Берковицкой нахій ѿсело

27

30

31

33

34

ѴСЕЕГО
ЖЕРБХ
ВАЛЬКО
ГРАДЕ

36

39

40

4

42

Ὁ ΖΑΧΑΡΙΑ Χ.
ΖΩΓΡΑΦΩ Τȣ ΕΝ.
CΑΜΟΚΟΒΙΟΝ.

ЗАХАРІЙ Х. ЗОГРАФ
БОЛГАРИНЪ.

ἘΖΩΓΡΑΦΕCΗ
ΔΙΑ ΧΗΡΩ Μȣ.

ЙЗОБРАЗЙ СА
РȣКОЮ МОЕЮ

43

45

46

47

48

49

НАНЕДЖЖНЫХРЖКЫВЪЗЛОЖЖТЪ·И
ЗДРАВИБЖДЖТЪ · ГЬЖЕIПОГЛАНН
НГОЕЖЕКЪНИМЪ · ВЪЗНЕСЕСАНАНЕ
БЕСА·ИСЪДЕОДЕСНЖЖБА · ОНИЖЕН
ШЕДШЕПРОПОВѢДААХЖ
ВЬСЖДОУ · ГОУПОСПѢШЬ
СТВОУЖШОУ · ИСЛОВООУТВРЬ
ЖДАЖШОУ · ПОСЛѢСТВОУЖ
ЦИИИИЗНАМЕНИИ. АМИН:

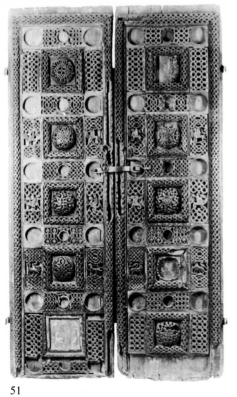

51

52

53

54

55

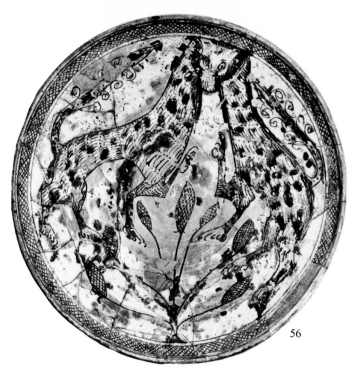

56

57

58

59

61

62

Notes on the Plates

1 Memorial stele of Anaxander, from Sozopol (Apollonia). Discovered in 1895, this marble stele is dated variously to the late sixth or early fifth century BC, and is a fine specimen of imported Greek work. Anaxander leans on his stick, and gazes down at his dog, which stretches up on its hind legs to accept something from his hand. According to Hoddinott (*Bulgaria in Antiquity*, p. 34), there is a stylistic resemblance to the stele from Orchomenos by Alexenor of Naxos. The treatment of the hair and drapery recall the Late Archaic style, but the peaceful realism and rhythmic composition bring it within the Classical tradition. Height 2.40 m. National Archaeological Museum, Sofia.

2, Portions of the painted ceiling of the
3 Thracian tomb at Kazanluk, in the Valley of the Roses. The tomb – that of an individual of princely rank and his wife – was discovered by chance in 1944, by soldiers digging an air-raid shelter in what was thought to be a natural hillock, 7 m. high and 40 m. in diameter. The brick-built, beehive-shaped inner chamber has a diameter of 2.65 and a height of

3.25 m. The paintings are in four colours, white, black, red and yellow. The scenes depicted in the dome form a composition of serene dignity and restrained sorrow, as well as providing insight into daily life in Bulgaria in the Hellenistic era. Late fourth or early third century BC.

4, The Madara Horseman. General
5 view of the cliff, with the carving, and close-up showing detail of the relief and the adjoining Greek inscriptions. These narrate important events in early Bulgarian history. The height of the relief is almost 3 m.; it stands over 25 m. above ground level. The whole work is an apotheosis of the might of the Sublime Khan of the Bulgars, and recalls prototypes in Sasanian Iran.

6 Pliska. Ruins of the royal basilica of Prince Boris-Michael, late ninth century. Including the cloistered atrium, the building was 99 m. long, and almost 30 m. wide.

7 Pliska. The Little Palace. Usually dated to the early eighth century, the Little Palace was a two-storey structure, with four large halls and a

number of smaller rooms on the ground floor.

8 Pliska. The Little Palace, heating installations. In both the Large Palace of Khan Omurtag (816–31) and the earlier Little Palace, the remains of bathrooms, hypocausts and other heating equipment were found. The discovery of extensive piping shows that the city of Pliska was well supplied with running water. Some scholars maintain that the proto-Bulgars were only 'squatters' on an earlier Roman or Byzantine site. However, Professor D. Obolensky (*The Byzantine Commonwealth*, p. 50) mentions that in AD 580, Bayan, khagan of the Avars, had baths built by Byzantine architects near Sirmium. Baths were also installed by 'Umay-yad caliphs in Syria a century later. The building of public and palace baths was a status symbol of successful dynasts in the Near Eastern and Byzantine spheres of influence throughout this period.

9 Stone inscribed with runic signs, from Biala, south of Varna. Proto-Bulgar period. Varna Archaeological Museum.

10 Proto-Bulgar pottery vessel, inscribed with runic signs. Height 26 cm. Varna Archaeological Museum.

11 Slavonic clay cooking-pot from Dev-

nya, the former Roman Marciano-polis, in the hinterland of Varna. Eighth-ninth century. Height 16 cm. Varna Archaeological Museum.

12 Gold treasure of Nagy Sankt Miklós (or Nagyszentmiklós), discovered in 1799 in the Romanian Banat. One of a pair of zoomorphic drinking cups or small bowls. Overall height 11 cm.; length 12.2 cm.; width 7 cm. Weight 284 gr. 20½ carats. Ref.: Mavrodinov, *Le Trésor protobulgare de Nagyszent-miklós*, 1943, nos. 13–14. Ninth century AD. Vienna: Kunsthistor-isches Museum.

13 Nagy Sankt Miklós treasure. Goblet decorated with six circular medal-lions, depicting various kinds of hippocampi or marine monsters. Height 5.7 cm.; diameter of mouth 6.2 cm.; diameter of base 5.3 cm.; body diameter 9 cm. Weight 217.5 gr. 22 carats. Mavrodinov, no. 19. Ninth century. Vienna: Kunsthistorisches Museum.

14, Nagy Sankt Miklós treasure. Gold
15 ewer (Mavrodinov, no. 2) and one of the four repoussé medallions which form part of its decoration. It shows a royal hunter mounted on a fantastic beast with a griffin's body and the head of a bearded man. The hunter has turned round in the saddle, and is shooting with his bow at a leaping

panther. Though imbued with the ferocious spirit of the barbarian nations, there are features strongly recalling Sasanian royal hunting scenes.

Height of ewer 22 cm.; overall diameter 14.5 cm.; diameter of base 8.4 cm.; diameter of mouth 5.8 cm. Weight 608 gr. 18 carats. Vienna: Kunsthistorisches Museum.

16 Nagy Sankt Miklós treasure. Gold ewer with handle. The medallion (there is a matching one on the other side of the vessel) shows the abduction of Ganymede by Zeus, disguised as an eagle. Ganymede, it will be remembered, was to serve as cup-bearer to the gods. The ewer has a flattened, ovoid contour. (Mavrodinov, no. 7.) Height 23 cm.; overall diameter 13 cm.; diameter of base 9 cm.; diameter of mouth 8.8 cm. Weight 733 gr. 21 carats. Vienna: Kunsthistorisches Museum.

17 Sofia. Church of St Sophia (in the foreground). Several times destroyed by barbarian invaders, the present brick-built church is probably the fifth to have been erected on this central site of the present Bulgarian capital. The city (formerly known as Serdica, then Sredets) takes its name from this church. Total length of present edifice, often ascribed to the reign of Justinian (6th century) is

46.5 m. See Hoddinott, *Bulgaria in Antiquity*, pp. 269-77, with diagrams, and plans of still earlier structures.

Behind, centre, can be seen the ostentatious golden-domed cathedral of Alexander Nevsky, built to celebrate the liberation of Bulgaria by Russia in 1877; in the crypt is a magnificent display of medieval Bulgarian art treasures.

18 Great Preslav. Royal palace of Tsar Symeon (893–927). Ruins of the reception hall, seen from northwest.

19 Great Preslav. Round or Golden Church of Tsar Symeon, c. AD 900. View of the ruins, showing the supporting wall.

20 Great Preslav. Round or Golden Church of Tsar Symeon. Detail of marble capital, showing a hare. There are parallels with contemporary sculpture in Armenia and Georgia. Height 24 cm. Preslav Museum.

21 Great Preslav. Carved decorative flagstone from the palace area, c. AD 900. 54 cm. × 96 cm. Marble. National Archaeological Museum, Sofia.

22 Silver goblet of the Great Zhupan Sivin, a high official at the Bulgarian court. Discovered in 1963 in a grave immediately north of Preslav. The goblet has a commemorative inscription in Greek on the base. c. AD 900.

Height 5.2 cm.; maximum diameter 9.2 cm.; diameter of base 5.2 cm. Preslav Museum.

23, Stone slabs with bas-reliefs, from
24 Stara Zagora. One shows a lion, perhaps a symbol of the might of the Bulgarian state; the other, a lioness and her cub. Probably tenth century. National Archaeological Museum, Sofia.

25 General view of the Rila monastery. The sanctuary was founded by St John of Rila (876–946), who originally lived in a hollow tree near by until the tree collapsed. Apart from Khrelyo's Tower, the original buildings were destroyed in a fire in 1833. Thus, the majority of the monastery buildings date from 1834 onwards.

26 The Rila monastery. Main courtyard, showing the massive Khrelyo's Tower (1335) with its crenellated parapet, designed for defence against invaders.

27 Nineteenth-century etching by an unknown artist, showing St John of Rila (left) together with St John the Theologian.

28 View of the main courtyard and principal church of the Bachkovo monastery. Most of the present monastery buildings date from the seventeenth century. The monastery was founded in 1083 by the Byzantine general Gregory Bakuriani and his brother, Abasi, and originally reserved for monks from Georgia in the Caucasus.

29 Two-storeyed church of the Petrich Virgin at Assen's Castle, between Assenovgrad and the Bachkovo monastery. Twelfth century. Overall dimensions 18 m. × 7 m.

30 Nessebăr. Church of St John the Baptist, dating from the tenth-eleventh century. View from southeast. Built of undressed stone, the church is cruciform in plan, 12 m. × 10 m., with tall cylindrical drum and three aisles. For this and the two following items, reference should be made to Veyrenc, *Nagel's Encyclopedia-Guide to Bulgaria*, pp. 292–304.

31 Nessebăr. Church of St Stephen. Detail of the upper section of the main apse, from outside. This basilica is also known as the Nova Mitropolia or New Metropolitan church, and has a series of fine medieval frescoes. Overall dimensions 15 m. × 9 m.

32 Nessebăr. Fourteenth-century church of the Pantocrator. The alternate layers of red brick and cut stone help to produce a splendid effect. Overall dimensions 16 m. × 6.70 m.

33 Vidin, on the river Danube. Baba Vida castle. The fortifications date originally from the thirteenth century, but were rebuilt in Ottoman times.

34 The crags of Belogradchik, in north/western Bulgaria, showing part of the medieval fortress, extended in Otto/man times.

35 Bachkovo monastery. Detail from a set of mural paintings, dating from about AD 1100, in the ossuary. This fresco of the Virgin Mary forms part of the Deesis scene, in the central apse.

36 Boyana church near Sofia. Part of the cycle of mural paintings, executed in 1259: detail from the section depict/ing Christ's descent into Hell. Just risen from the dead, the three proph/ets David, Melchizedek and Solo/mon are shown standing in their sarcophagi, while St John the Baptist behind them holds an open scroll with prophetic utterance about the coming of Christ.

37 Boyana church murals: Christ as Pantocrator.

38 Boyana church murals: St Theodore Tyro.

39 Cliffs beside the river Rusenski Lom, in northeastern Bulgaria, close to the village of Ivanovo. During the four/

teenth century, in the reign of Tsar Ivan Alexander, the Turkish peril forced the monks to take refuge in rock/cut churches and cells, perched high up in cliff faces such as these.

40 Ivanovo. Entrance to the rock/cut monastery church.

41 Ivanovo. Detail of the cycle of four/teenth/century frescoes in the monas/tery church. One section shows the events of Holy Week and Christ's Crucifixion and Resurrection. This is part of the scene of Christ washing the feet of the Disciples. Despite the worn state of the fresco, we can still discern the subtle and skilful treat/ment of the Disciples' robes, and the effect of bustle and bewilderment as the Disciples protest their unworthi/ness to receive Christ's ministrations.

42 Ivanovo murals: Judas Iscariot (right) returns the blood money to the Phari/sees (Gospel of St Matthew, XXVII, 3–5). The impact of this scene is heightened by the use of sinister dark green shades. The agitated figure of the repentant Judas is contrasted with the complacent figures of the seated Pharisees. Note the interesting treat/ment of the temple buildings in the background. The panel measures 93 cm. × 148 cm.

43 Self/portrait of the illustrious painter Zakhari Zograf (1810–53), one of

the greatest figures of the Bulgarian renaissance of the nineteenth century. His arresting and often humorous murals adorn the chief monastery churches of Bulgaria, also the Great Lavra of St Athanasius on Mt Athos. This self-portrait dates from 1840, and is painted on the church of St Nicholas, Bachkovo.

44 Bachkovo monastery: church of the Archangels. Fresco by Zakhari Zograf, 'The rich man's death', part of a group of murals in the porch. Painted in 1841.

45 Preslav. Patleina monastery. Icon of St Theodore Stratelates, made up of twenty glazed ceramic tiles, each 11.5 cm. square. Basic colours are gold, light brown and greenish black. About AD 900. Preslav Museum.

46 Icon of St Arsenius, fourteenth century. The colouring is an effective blend of shades of pink and red, set off by the white of the saint's vestments and hair and beard. Monastery Museum, Rila.

47 Icon of the Virgin and Child, from Nessebăr. Fourteenth century. Sofia: National Archaeological Museum.

48 The Adoration of the Magi, from the personal Gospel book of Tsar Ivan

Alexander, copied by the Monk Symeon in 1355–56. British Library, Add. MS. 39627. f. 10: on exhibition in the British Museum.

49 The conversion and baptism of the Russians. Miniature from the Slavonic recension of the chronicle of Constantine Manasses (died 1187). Copied 1344–45. Vatican Library.

50 Illuminated page from the Gospels of Tsar Ivan Alexander. Above, the Ascension; below, Tsar Ivan Alexander converses with St Mark the Evangelist. British Museum.

51 Carved wooden double door from Khrelyo's Tower, in the Rila Monastery. About 1335. 1.22 m. × 2.03 m. Monastery Museum, Rila.

52 Gold belt tag, with inset stones framing a female figure. Fourteenth century. Found on the Tsarevets hill (acropolis), Great Tărnovo. Regional Historical Museum, Great Tărnovo.

53 Gold belt buckle, with inset stones framing a winged dragon figure. Fourteenth century. From the Tsarevets hill. Regional Historical Museum, Great Tărnovo.

54 Medallion representing two lions. Bronze with enamel inlay. Fourteenth century. From the Tsarevets

hill. Regional Historical Museum, Great Tărnovo.

55 Silver coin of Tsar Ivan Alexander, showing (obverse) the ruler with Prince Michael Assen, and (reverse) standing figure of Christ. This series was struck between 1331 and 1355. Average diameter 20 mm.; average weight between 1.30 and 1.75 gr. Barber Institute of Fine Arts, University of Birmingham.

56 Shallow bowl in sgraffito ware, found on Tsarevets acropolis. Depicted are two fantastic heraldic beasts, sharing a single head. Thirteenth/fourteenth century. Diameter 34 cm. Regional Historical Museum, Great Tărnovo.

57 The carved wooden ceiling of the Daskalov House in Tryavna, a masterpiece of the Tryavna school of carving. Incorporating a symbolic depiction of the July sun, the ceiling dates from 1808.

58 The Fall: Adam and Eve being expelled by the angel from the Garden of Eden. Part of the Little Iconostasis in the church of the Rozhen monastery. Height of the angel 14 cm. Box wood. Seventeenth century.

59 Detail from the scene of Abraham entertaining the Angels. Another section from the Little Iconostasis at Rozhen. Height of Abraham's figure 15 cm.

60 The Virgin and Child. Part of the iconostasis in the semi/underground church of the Virgin at Pazarjik, dating from 1837. This iconostasis is a masterpiece of the craftsmen of the Debăr school.

61 Kukeri dancers and mummers. Their fantastic costume, and the fertility rites which the Kukeri groups celebrate, are thought to derive ultimately from Thracian times.

62 The rebeck player – a type of traditional village musician still frequently encountered in the Balkan countryside.

Index

Note: Countries and peoples occurring repeatedly in the text, e.g. Balkans, Bulgaria, Slavs, have not been included in this index.

Index

Index

Index